LUTHER ON EDUCATION

INCLUDING

A HISTORICAL INTRODUCTION

AND

A TRANSLATION OF THE REFORMER'S TWO MOST IMPORTANT EDUCATIONAL TREATISES.

BY

F. V. N. PAINTER, A. M.,

Professor of Modern Languages in Roanoke College, and Author of a "History of Education."

St. Louis, Mo.
CONCORDIA PUBLISHING HOUSE.

PRINTED IN U. S. A.

PREFACE.

THIS little work illustrates the growth of an idea. It began with the translation of the "Letter to the Mayors and Aldermen of all the Cities of Germany in behalf of Christian Schools," of which a perusal a few years ago had led me to say in my "History of Education:" "If we consider its pioneer character, in connection with its statement of principles and admirable recommendations, the address must be regarded the most important educational treatise ever written." The translation of the "Sermon on the Duty of Sending Children to School," the most elaborate of Luther's educational writings, naturally followed as presenting more fully the great Reformer's views. The interest thus awakened led to an examination of all that he had written about education, and to an attempt to arrange in a somewhat systematic form his educational opinions and principles. The fact that no great character can be fully understood without an acquaintance with the age in which he lived and the movements with which he was identified, led to the preparation of the first four chapters as a historical introduction.

The justification of the work must be found partly in the interest and value of Luther's views, and partly in the relation of those views to educational progress. Though it is not generally recognized, yet Luther brought about as important a reformation in education as in religion. With his earnest nature and profound penetration he laid hold of fundamental facts and principles that are often neglected in the rapid movements of the present. The progress of our century in education—a progress that constitutes no small part of its pre-eminence—has its roots in the principles and labors of the German reformer. This fact, it is believed, renders the present work a not untimely contribution to our excellent and rapidly increasing educational literature.

The two treatises of Luther contained in this work have never before appeared in English. The translation is made from the Leipsic edition of Luther's works. A judicious medium between a literal and a periphrastic rendering has been aimed at, but it is not easy to make the great, rugged, impetuous German speak our language acceptably. Except the passages from his Catechisms, of which there are several good translations, nearly all the extracts illustrating the Reformer's educational views have been taken directly from the German. Whenever an extract has been thought of especial importance, a reference has been given to its source; but in most cases this has not been deemed necessary.

F. V. N. PAINTER.

Salem, Virginia, September 5, 1889.

CONTENTS.

CHAPTER I.
CAUSES OF THE REFORMATION 9

CHAPTER II.
THE PAPACY AND POPULAR EDUCATION 32

CHAPTER III.
PROTESTANTISM AND POPULAR EDUCATION 52

CHAPTER IV.
EDUCATION BEFORE THE REFORMATION 75

CHAPTER V.
LUTHER 90

CHAPTER VI.
LUTHER ON DOMESTIC TRAINING 113

CHAPTER VII.
LUTHER ON SCHOOLS 128

CHAPTER VIII.
LUTHER ON STUDIES AND METHODS 147

CONTENTS.

CHAPTER IX.

LETTER TO THE MAYORS AND ALDERMEN OF THE CITIES OF GERMANY IN BEHALF OF CHRISTIAN SCHOOLS . . 169

CHAPTER X.

SERMON ON THE DUTY OF SENDING CHILDREN TO SCHOOL 210

LUTHER ON EDUCATION.

CHAPTER I.

CAUSES OF THE REFORMATION.

THE greatest achievement of the Germanic race, and the most important event in history since the advent of Christ, is the Reformation of the sixteenth century. Though involving a multitude of interests, it was essentially a religious movement, which sought to correct the errors in doctrine and practice that had crept into the Church. In connection with coöperating influences presently to be noticed, the Reformation began a new stage in human progress; it marks the close of the Middle Ages, and the dawn of the modern era. Insignificant in its beginning, it appealed so strongly to the conscience of the Teutonic nations that it speedily assumed a world-wide significance. There is scarcely an important human interest that it has not affected. It has secured greater purity and spirituality in religion; it has contributed to the elevation of the laity and the advancement of woman; it has confirmed the separation of the secular and the ecclesiastical power; it has given an extraordinary impulse to literature and science; it has established the right of liberty of conscience; in a word, it is closely related to all that distinguishes and ennobles our modern civilization.

The Reformation has long been a subject of controversy; and at the present time, because of recent Roman Catholic attacks, its origin and significance are being investigated with renewed interest. In many of the discussions of the past, ignorance, prejudice, and passion have led to one-sided statements, and to erroneous or inadequate explanations. There have been writers of high rank, as Hume and Voltaire, who have alleged the rivalry between the Augustinian and the Dominican friars as the origin of the Reformation. "You are not unaware," says the Frenchman, "that this great revolution in the human mind and in the political system of Europe began with Martin Luther, an Augustinian monk, whom his superiors deputed to preach against the traffic in indulgences which had been refused them. The quarrel was at first between the Augustinians and the Dominicans."* The state-

---

*Voltaire, Essai sur les Moeurs, chapter 127.

ments made in the latter part of this extract are wholly without foundation.

The Roman Catholic view has the merit of great simplicity. The Reformation was a rebellion against the Church. Luther, the arch-heretic, or, as Audin calls him, "the Sampson of the Reformation," led the revolt, and gathered about him all the elements of discontent existing in the social and the religious world. "He arbitrarily set himself up as a reformer of the Church, inveighed against the ecclesiastical authorities, especially against the Pope, whose supreme power he denounced as usurpation and tyranny. . . In pursuance of his wrong views, he rejected many articles of faith which the Church had received from Christ and his apostles. He discarded the holy sacrifice of the mass, fasting, confession, prayers for the dead, and many other pious practices; he declared good works to be useless, and taught that man is justified and saved by faith alone. . . Luther boasted that he took his doctrine from the Bible only; but being misled by the false rule of private judgment in its interpretation, he soon fell into the most palpable contradictions and errors. . . Nevertheless he soon obtained many followers; for the thoughtless multitude were very much pleased with such easy doctrine, which allowed them to lead a dissolute life, and covetous princes found nothing more conformable to their wishes than the suppression of churches and monasteries."* Apart from the many erroneous statements contained in this passage, particularly in reference to the uselessness of good works, and the dissoluteness of life encouraged by the "easy doctrines" of Protestantism, the explanation of the reformatory movement is exceedingly inadequate and biased.

1. Among the several coöperating causes of the Reformation now to be considered, a prominent place must be given to the effort of the human mind in Europe to throw off the oppressive intellectual tyranny of the Papacy. The Reformation, says Guizot, "was a vast effort made by the human mind to achieve its freedom; it was a new-born desire which it felt, to think and judge freely and independently of facts and opinions which till then Europe received, or was considered bound to receive, from the hands of authority. It was a great endeavor to emancipate human reason; and, to call things by their right names, it was an insurrection of the human mind against the absolute power of the spiritual order."†

---

* A Full Catechism of the Catholic Religion, by the Rev. Joseph Deharbe, S. J. Twelfth American Edition. Imprimatur of N. Card. Wiseman, and of John Card. McCloskey.

† Guizot, History of Civilization. Chapter XII.

The correctness and significance of this explanation of the reformatory movement will appear upon a brief survey of the facts. At the opening of the sixteenth century, the human mind in Europe had attained a higher plane of intelligence than it had occupied for a thousand years. This result was brought about by many remarkable circumstances. The revival of classical learning, which had its central point in the downfall of Constantinople in 1453, exerted a strong and pervading influence. It opened the literary treasures of Greece and Rome—the richest fruitage of heathen intellect—and awakened Europe with its new and higher form of culture. The invention of gunpowder wrought an important and salutary change in society. It weakened the influence and power of the knightly order, which had hitherto been preëminent in military operations, and by placing a powerful weapon in the hands of the lower classes, it gradually led to an amelioration of their condition. The discovery of America and of a sea-passage to the East Indies, led to numerous voyages of exploration, quickened commercial activity, and made large contributions to the general store of knowledge. In the cities an influential middle class, or "third estate," composed of merchants and artisans, won recognition at the hands of the nobility and the clergy—the two orders that had been preëminent during the reign of feudalism. The rise of the universities, beginning with that of Bologna in the twelfth century, stimulated intellectual pursuits, and promoted the diffusion of knowledge. The invention of printing, which at once supplanted the tedious and costly process of copying books by hand, multiplied the sources of knowledge, and brought them within reach of a larger circle of readers. These circumstances harmoniously worked together in lifting Europe to a higher intellectual plane, and in making the people restive under an ecclesiastical tutelage which, in matters of supreme importance, forbade, under fearful penalties, all independence of thought and judgment.

2. Another cause of the Reformation is found in the unbelief, ignorance, worldliness, and vice, that characterized many representatives of the Papacy at that period. Attempts have been made by recent Roman Catholic writers to reconstruct the accepted history of that age, and to gloss over the corrupt condition of the Church. But a careful investigation of the subject amply justifies the rise of Protestantism, and shows that the precious heritage of existing freedom and culture is not the result of a tremendous error.

"The Reformation," says Hegel, "resulted from the *corruption of the Church.*"* While there were many

---

* Hegel, Philosophy of History.

devout and intelligent Christians in the Church (a fact that should not be forgotten), its general condition, from the Pope down to the humblest sexton, was a reproach to its divine Founder. The spiritual conception of the Church had been lost. It had been gradually transformed into a vast external organization, officered by the Pope and his subordinates, and used by them for selfish and sensual ends. At the court of Rome, in the midst of excessive outward splendor, there existed a spirit of unbelief and licentiousness. The remark that Leo X. is said to have made to his secretary Bembo accords well with the prevailing spirit in the pontifical palace: "All the world knows how profitable this fable of Christ has been to us and ours."* The wide-spread infidelity led the tenth Lateran Council to establish the doctrine of the immortality of the soul by a special decree. When Luther was dispatched to Rome as the envoy of the Augustine brotherhood, he was one day at table with several distinguished prelates, whose conversation, as he tells us, was impious. Among other things, they boasted that at mass, instead of the sacramental words, they mockingly pronounced over the elements, "Bread thou art, and bread thou shalt remain; wine thou art,

---

* D'Aubigné, History of the Reformation, Book 1, Chapter 7, where the original source is given.

and wine thou shalt remain." Blasphemy was never more shameless. Ardor for antiquity became intoxication, and the paganism of Athens was revived in Christian Rome. The simple language of the Scripture became offensive to the devotees of the classics, and its sublime truths were subject to outrageous parody. The Holy Ghost was written "the breath of the heavenly zephyr," and the expression to forgive sins was rendered "to bend the manes and the sovereign gods." Alexander VI. was a monster of impiety. During his reign the Vatican became the scene of treachery and murder, and the dissolute entertainments given in the pontifical palace surpassed the groves of antiquity in horrible licentiousness.

As the head, so the members. The bishops lived in the midst of splendor, and squandered in sensual pleasures the revenues of the Church. In seeking to extend their authority, they were frequently at war with cities and princes. Ecclesiastical offices were bought and sold, and children were raised to episcopal dignity. The secular clergy or priests were coarse and ignorant, and through the unnatural law of celibacy, they became exceedingly corrupt in morals. They fell into disrepute with the common people, who ridiculed them in songs and pictures; and for a century or longer they were the notorious targets for the shafts of satirists.

Of the monasteries frightful pictures are given by writers of the time. The following portrayal, given by John Schiphower, himself a monk, is not more condemning than innumerable others that have been left us. After speaking of the shamelessness of the monks in preaching and in controversy, he continues: "The manner in which they lived their lives is equally objectionable. They much better understood how to draw liquor from goblets than information from books. With drinking and carousing companions, they sit in taverns, carry on games and illicit amours, and daily intoxicate themselves. And these are—priests! they are indeed so called, but they are—brutes."* In this sad state of the Church, which has not been too darkly depicted, was found a strong appeal for reformatory measures.

3. Another cause of the Reformation is found in the external character imposed upon religion by the Papacy. The legalism and ceremonial of the Old Testament were substituted for the grace and spiritual worship of the New Testament. The religion of Christ consists essentially in a personal relation to him—a relation of faith, love and obedience. Salvation is not something earned by human effort, but a gift proceeding from the infinite love of God. The

---

* Tischer, Life of Luther.

will of the believer is brought into harmony with the divine will. The Christian enjoys constant communion with God, to whom he has immediate access through Christ. By the profound reverence and obedient love begotten of faith, men become the sons of God, the recipients of all the privileges and blessings pertaining to a filial relation. The kingdom of God in the world is composed of the collective body of believers—a kingdom, not of outward pomp and splendor, but of inward purity, love, and obedience. The written Word of God is its law. In this kingdom, every longing of our nature finds complete satisfaction, and human nature is unspeakably ennobled, not only by the filial relation it sustains to God, but also by the pure affections that reign in the heart.

All this was perverted by the Papacy. The spiritual kingdom of Christ was supplanted by an outward kingdom, presided over by a succession of ecclesiastical princes. The Pope, as the vicar of Christ, stood at its head. Everything pertaining to the kingdom—doctrine, government, and worship—received an external character. The representatives of the Church surrounded themselves with regal magnificence. In order to maintain this splendor, the laity were burdened with numberless pecuniary exactions. Says Martin Meyer, a chancellor at Mayence in 1457: "A thousand ways are devised, by which the Romish chair cunningly robs us poor barbarians of money. And thus it has come about that our nation, once so highly renowned, and which by its courage and blood set up the Roman empire, and rose to be mistress and queen of the world, has now been reduced to a poor, servile, and tributary condition, and for many years has been groveling in the mire, and deploring her misfortune and poverty."* Opposition of every kind was put down by force. Kings were dethroned, as in the case of John of England, and Henry IV. of Germany; reformers, like Huss and Jerome of Prague, were burned; and communities of a purer religious faith and practice, like the Albigenses, were exterminated by fire and sword. The mass, in which the consecrated elements are offered to God as a sacrifice for the living and the dead, became the central point in worship. The preaching of the truth, through which men's hearts and lives are transformed, fell into disuse. By means of indulgences, sin could in a measure be compounded for with money. The distinguishing features of a religious life were not love and obedience to God, but pilgrimages, flagellations, and fastings. Religion became a thing of outward observances, not of inward piety. Myconius, who was long a monk,

---

* Ullmann, Reformers before the Reformation, Vol. I., 194.

but afterwards a fellow-laborer of Luther's, has given a graphic picture of the religious life of the period: "The sufferings and merit of Christ were looked upon as an idle tale, or as the fictions of Homer. There was no thought of the faith by which we become partakers of the Saviour's righteousness and of the heritage of eternal life. Christ was looked upon as a severe judge, prepared to condemn all who should not have recourse to the intercession of the saints, or to the papal indulgences. Other intercessors appeared in his place; first the Virgin Mary, like the Diana of paganism, and then the saints, whose numbers were continually augmented by the Popes. These mediators granted their intercession only to such applicants as had deserved well of the Orders founded by them. For this it was necessary to do, not what God had commanded in his Word, but to perform a number of works invented by monks and priests, and which brought money to the treasury. These works were Ave Marias, the prayers of Saint Ursula and of Saint Bridget: they must chant and cry night and day. There were as many resorts for pilgrims as there were mountains, forests, and valleys. But these penances might be compounded for with money. The people, therefore, brought to the convents and to the priests money and everything that had any value—fowls, ducks, geese, eggs, wax, straw, butter and cheese. Then the hymns resounded, the bells rang, incense filled the sanctuary, sacrifices were offered up, the larder overflowed, the glasses went round, and masses terminated and concealed these pious orgies. The bishops no longer preached, but they consecrated priests, bells, monks, churches, chapels, images, books, and cemeteries; and all this brought in a large revenue. Bones, arms, and feet were preserved in gold and silver boxes; they were given out during mass for the faithful to kiss, and this, too, was a source of great profit."*

It is not to be denied that in the externalism of which we have been speaking, there was something adapted to an uncultivated age, incapable of high spiritual emotion. The Papacy may be regarded as a natural historical development, though embodying an error destined to work its ruin. A special priestly class was helpful in administering the affairs of the Church, and in governing the lawlessness of an undisciplined people. An imposing ritual served to inspire religious awe at a time when simpler ministrations might have left the heart untouched. But at the period of the Reformation, the Teutonic nations had

---

*Myconius, History of the Reformation. This extract is taken from D'Aubigné. Myconius was held in high esteem by Luther and Melancthon.

outgrown this externalism, and apart from its abuses they began to long for something higher and better. Their deep religious nature, no longer satisfied with forms and symbols, demanded a spiritual Christianity, in which the soul might be united with God, and life in its ordinary duties be sanctified as a divine service. This feeling found expression in the mystics of the fourteenth century, who were characterized by an inward piety. It was manifested also at the reformatory Councils of Constance and Basel. It is found in the writings of such men as Wyclif and Huss, and also, on a larger scale, in the doctrine and practice of the Waldenses. When at length Luther proposed a return to the Christianity of the New Testament, he had the support of Germany.

4. Another cause of the Reformation is found in the pretensions of the Papacy to temporal power, and in the growth of a national feeling in the several countries of Europe. The Papacy, as it existed at the time of the Reformation, was the result of a development extending through many centuries. Step by step, from the congregational polity of the apostolic church, the episcopal power increased, until under Gregory VII., in the eleventh century, it reached its climax in the universal supremacy of the Roman pontiff. "The world," says Gregory, "is governed

by two lights—by the sun, which is greater, and by the moon, which is less. The apostolic power is the sun; the royal power, the moon. For as the latter has its light from the former, so do emperors, and kings, and princes, receive power through the Pope, who receives it from God. Thus the power of the Roman chair is greater than the power of the throne, and the king is subordinate to the Pope, and bound to obey him."* The Papacy, as we see, aimed at a theocracy, in which the pontiff, as vicar of Christ, was to possess universal dominion. This power was not simply theoretical, but also practical. In the long conflicts between the Popes and the sovereigns of Europe, it was frequently exercised. The Roman pontiff seated and dethroned kings. He placed nations under the ban, cutting off every religious privilege and comfort. He sought to exempt ecclesiastics, no matter how flagrant their crimes, from secular jurisdiction. He acquired temporal dominion, interfered with secular authority, formed political alliances, waged cruel wars.

But while the Papacy was at the very height of its power, a mighty influence was slowly but surely

---

* This is a famous passage. It is found in various church histories. As here given, it is translated from Kohlrausb, *Deutsche Geschichte*.

undermining its authority. From various causes, the several nations of Europe—Germany, France, Spain, England—were acquiring a strong self-consciousness. It was a part of that general progress manifest in all Europe toward the close of the Middle Ages. In every country a spirit of patriotism was awakened—a spirit that opposed all interference on the part of a foreign prince, even when clothed with supreme ecclesiastical dignity. Papal pecuniary exactions met with increasing opposition; papal bulls were sometimes disregarded or resisted; reverence for the Pope as head of the Church declined among princes and people. Louis XII., of France, had a medal struck with the inscription, "*Perdam Babylonis nomen*—I will destroy the name of Babylon." Maximilian, of Austria, speaking of Leo X., by whom he had been deceived, said, "This Pope also, in my opinion, is a scoundrel. I may now say that never in my life has any Pope kept his faith or his word with me." During the so-called Babylonish captivity of the Papacy at Avignon, in the fourteenth century, its sympathy with French interests, and its subserviency to French kings, intensified this national feeling against the Popes. The literary mind in the several countries of Europe led a reaction against Roman domination. The vernacular languages, which toward the close of the Middle Ages began to assume a literary form, were made the media of sharp and unceasing attacks upon the avarice, tyranny, and degeneracy of the papal hierarchy. Walther von der Vogelweide, the best of the Minnesingers of the thirteenth century, says that "the Pope himself increases infidelity, for he leads the clergy by the devil's rein; they are full of vices, they do not practice what they preach, and he who is a Christian in words only, and not in deeds, is really half a heathen." In the Prologue to the Canterbury Tales, Chaucer, along with an inimitable portrait of a faithful village pastor, depicts the coarse sensuality of a friar, and the shallow fraud of a pardoner or indulgence vender:

> "Whose walet lay biforn hym in his lappe
> Brimful of pardon, come from Rome all hot.
> * * * * *
> But of his craft, fro Berwyk unto Ware
> Ne was there such another pardoner;
> For in his male[1] he had a pilwebeer[2]
> Which, that he seyde, was oure lady veyl;
> He said he had a gobet[3] of the seyl
> Thatte St. Peter hadde whan that he wente
> Upon the sea, til Jhesu Crist hym hente.[4]
> He had a croys of latoun[5] full of stones
> And in a glas he hadde pigges bones."

---

[1] Valise. [2] Pillow-case. [3] Piece. [4] Took.
[5] A kind of tinned iron.

Thus, on every hand, was gathering a storm that needed only a favorable opportunity to burst upon Rome.

5. Behind all these causes we must not forget the providence of God. He is ever present in the great movements of succeeding generations. Though His presence is unrecognized by the heedless multitude, it becomes manifest to the devout inquirer who, turning away from the distracting turmoil of human events, seeks in all things an ultimate cause and an intelligent purpose. God in history is a great fact, an invaluable lesson coming to us from the Old Testament, a mighty truth that gathers up what is seemingly fragmentary in human affairs, and binds them together in the symmetry of a majestic temple. Not alone for the advent of Christ, but for every significant epoch in the world's progress, there is a "fullness of time." The history of mankind is not a chaos. The hand of God is especially manifest in the Reformation. The favoring circumstances that we have considered, were not, as some believe, a fortuitous concurrence, but an intelligent preparation for a new era of human advancement.

When everything was ready, the reformatory work began. Its immediate occasion was Tetzel's sale of indulgences. According to the Romish faith, "an indulgence is a remission of that temporal punishment which, even after the sin is forgiven, we have yet to undergo, either here or in purgatory."

The Church, it is claimed, has an inexhaustible treasure of the merits of Christ and his saints, which the Pope can draw upon at any time to make up deficiencies in individual members. At the time of the Reformation, this doctrine had given rise to gross abuses. This fact was recognized by the Council of Trent, which, after declaring that the use of indulgences should be retained in the Church, continues in its decree: "Nevertheless, the Council desires that moderation be shown in granting them, according to the ancient and approved custom of the Church, lest by too much laxity ecclesiastical discipline be weakened. Anxious moreover *to correct and amend the abuses* that have crept in, and by reason of which the honorable name of indulgences is blasphemed by the heretics, the Council determines generally by this present decree, that all wicked gains accruing from them, which have been the principal source of these abuses, shall be wholly abolished."* The abuses "proceeding from superstition, ignorance, and irreverence" are referred by the Council to the several bish-

---

* Smets, Concilii Tridentini, Sessio XXV. Schaff. Creeds of Christendom, Vol. II.

ops. Let us inquire a little more closely into the nature of these abuses.

In order to provide funds for the completion of St. Peter's at Rome, Leo X. had ordered a sale of indulgences. In 1517 John Tetzel, acting as agent for Albert, elector of Mayence, appeared at Jüterbock, not far from Wittenberg, and proceeded to dispose of his wares. Shrewd and unscrupulous, he extolled the virtue of indulgences in a shameless and even blasphemous manner. "His red cross with the Pope's arms," Tetzel said, "was as efficacious as the cross of Christ. In heaven he would not exchange places with St. Peter, for he had saved more souls with his indulgences than the apostle had saved with his gospel. The grace of indulgences was precisely the grace by which man was reconciled with God. Sorrow for sin was not necessary when an indulgence was bought; and as soon as the money rattled in the chest, the soul leaped from purgatory into heaven. Such great grace and power had been conferred upon him at Rome, that if any one had done violence to the Virgin Mary, he could forgive it, together with future sins, if the offender paid a sufficient sum of money."* Without re-

---

* Matthesius, Leben Luther's, Zweites Predigt. See also Meurer, Life of Luther, and D'Aubigné, History of Reformation.

pentance, all the penalties of sin were removed, and heaven was gained by money. Tetzel had even fixed a scale of prices for particular sins. For polygamy the charge was six ducats; for sacrilege and perjury, nine ducats; for murder, eight ducats; for witchcraft, two ducats. Such were some of the abuses of this infamous traffic.

Luther at this time was a professor, preacher, and pastor at Wittenberg. In the confessional, some of his people who had attended Tetzel's auction acknowledged gross sins—adultery, licentiousness, usury, ill-gotten gains; and when Luther sought to correct them, they refused to amend their lives. They appealed to their indulgences, which Luther would not recognize; and in the language of the Scripture he declared unto them, " Except ye repent, ye shall all likewise perish." Having thus seen the demoralizing effect of indulgences upon the religious life, and having also learned of Tetzel's blasphemous pretensions, he prepared ninety-five theses or propositions which were aimed at the abuses of the traffic, but which in reality undermined the doctrine of indulgences itself. "When our Lord and Master Jesus Christ said, Repent ye, etc., he meant that the whole earthly life of believers should be a repentance (Thesis 1)... The Pope has neither the will nor the power to remit any penalties, except those which he has imposed by his own authority, or by that of the canons of the Church (5)... Those preachers of indulgences are in error who say that, by the indulgences of the Pope, a man is loosed and saved from all punishment (21)... They preach the vain fancies of man, who say that the soul flies out of purgatory as soon as the money rattles in the chest (27)... Those who believe that through letters of pardon they are made sure of their own salvation, will be eternally damned along with their teachers (32). We must especially beware of those who say that these pardons from the Pope are that inestimable gift of God, by which man is reconciled to God (33)... They preach no Christian doctrine who teach that sorrow or repentance is not necessary for those who buy souls out of purgatory, or buy confessional licenses (35). Every Christian who truly repents of his sins has of right plenary remission of pain and guilt, even without letters of pardon (36)... To say that the cross set up among the insignia of the papal arms is of equal power with the cross of Christ, is blasphemy (79)."

These theses were nailed on the door of the church of All Saints, at Wittenberg, Oct. 31, 1517, and Luther offered to defend them against all comers. A papal agent and an accepted doctrine were attacked. In the issue thus joined, the Reformation had its beginning.

Summing up the results of this inquiry, we may say that the Reformation was due chiefly to the following co-operative causes:

1. A reaction, brought about by the increased intelligence of the people, against ecclesiastical oppression.

2. The corrupt condition of the Church in doctrine and practice.

3. The external character imposed upon Christianity by the Papacy.

4. The pretensions of the Popes to temporal power in the presence of a growing national spirit.

5. Back of these causes, the providence of God, which arranged the "fullness of time," and raised up the proper agent.

CHAPTER II.

THE PAPACY AND POPULAR EDUCATION.

THE Papacy must be distinguished from the Roman Catholic Church. According to authoritative Catholic standards, the Church is composed of all the faithful who have been baptized, profess the same doctrine, partake of the same sacraments, and are governed by one visible head, the Pope. Accepting this definition, external and defective as it is, we cheerfully recognize in the Roman Catholic communion the existence of evangelical piety. At the present time, as in the past, it contains many God-fearing men and women. The Papacy is the governing power of the Church. In its aims and methods, and in some of its teachings, even when administered by pious men, it is mischievous, tyrannical, and anti-Christian. It is the relation of the Papacy to popular education that is to be considered. While the Roman Church as a whole entertains the same views, it is not primarily responsible for them. The Church simply obeys the orders of its official leaders.

The Papacy, with all its boasted unity, has not always been at one with itself. Two antagonistic views have existed for centuries in regard to the powers of the See of Rome. The Gallican or episcopal view, represented by many distinguished prelates and defended by the Councils of Constance and Basel, makes the Church the ultimate source of authority. The Pope is but the administrative head of the Church. The Church finds utterance in its General Councils, which are superior to the Pope, and competent to pass laws binding upon him. This view restricts the Pope's jurisdiction to spiritual things, and forbids his interference in political affairs. It harmonizes papal supremacy with national independence. It is called Gallican, because its exemplification and its leading advocates as Gerson and Bossuet, were found in France.

The opposite of Gallicanism is Ultramontanism. The Ultramontane view makes the Pope the vicar of Christ on earth. As such he is the source of all power, both spiritual and temporal. The Church is under his absolute control. In his official utterances, he is incapable of erring. Princes are bound to obey him; and when he deems it desirable for the interests of the Church, he may resist or depose them. All episcopal authority is derived from him. It is his prerogative to call Councils, to watch over their proceedings, and to give validity to their decrees. He is the universal teacher of the Church, the authoritative interpreter of Scripture, and the source of all doctrine. When the decree of papal infallibility was passed by the Vatican Council in 1870, Ultramontanism was given a permanent ascendency. On this line the Roman Church is now working out its destiny. It is the purpose of the Papacy to secure universal supremacy; and it is this fact that renders it a constant menace and danger to existing institutions.

The organization of the Church, which embodies the practical wisdom of ages, is exceedingly compact. The laity are bound to obey the priest; the priest, the bishop; and the bishop, the Pope. This arrangement is supported in a surprising manner by doctrines, oaths, and penalties, and is designed to give the Pope absolute control of the clergy and laity throughout the world.

In the "Dogmatic Decrees of the Vatican Council" of 1870, it is said that "all the faithful of Christ must believe that the holy Apostolic See and the Roman pontiff possesses *the primacy over the world*, and that the Roman pontiff is the successor of the blessed Peter, Prince of Apostles, and is the true vicar of Christ, and head of the whole Church, and father and teacher of all Christians; and that full power was given to him in blessed Peter to rule, feed, and govern the universal

Church by Jesus Christ our Lord." A careful reading of these decrees in the light of history fully justifies Mr. Gladstone's judgment, that they "in the strictest sense establish for the Pope supreme command over loyal and civil duty."* Every Catholic layman, whether he realizes it or not, is bound by his connection with the Church to yield in all things obedience to the Pope. His ballot and the education of his children are subject to the Roman pontiff. In view of these facts, Bismarck was right when he said in 1875, "This Pope, this foreigner, this Italian, is more powerful in this country than any one person, not excepting even the King."

The authority of the Pope over the clergy is confirmed by an oath. After requiring fidelity and obedience to the Roman pontiff, the form of oath continues: "The rights, honors, privileges and authority of the holy Roman Church, of our lord the Pope, and his aforesaid successors, I will endeavor to preserve, defend, increase, and advance. I will not be in any counsel, action, or treaty, in which shall be plotted against our said lord, and the said Roman Church, any thing to the hurt or prejudice of their persons, rights, honor, state, or power; and if I shall know of any such thing to be treated by any whatsoever, I will

---

* Vaticanism, p. 7.

hinder it to my power; and as soon as I can, I will signify it to our said lord, or to some other, by whom it may come to his knowledge . . . Heretics, schismatics, and rebels to our said lord or his aforesaid successors, I will to my power persecute and oppose."* The Constitution of the United States forbids the establishment of a state religion, and guarantees liberty of conscience, and freedom of the press. Our naturalization laws require that "the alien seeking to be naturalized shall make oath that he will support the Constitution of the United States, and that he absolutely and entirely renounces and abjures all allegiance and fidelity to every foreign prince, potentate, or sovereignty, particularly the state or sovereignty of which he has been a subject." Our institutions are opposed to the principles of the Papacy. No Roman prelate of foreign birth can take the naturalization oath without perjury or disloyalty to the Pope. In holding to Ultramontanism, the Roman clergy of this country are a body of aliens, whose principles are at war with American institutions.

The doctrines and discipline of the Roman Church

---

* Pontificale Romanum. The last sentence in the original reads: "Haereticos, Schismaticos et Rebelles eidem Domino nostro vel successoribus praedictis pro posse persequar et impugnabo."

are marvelously adapted to maintain and perpetuate the power of the Papacy. A hierarchy is established between the laity and God—a hierarchy through which as a channel salvation is communicated. The sacrifice of the mass is the central thing in worship. By means of this sacrifice, the priest makes an offering to God for the sins of the living and the dead. According to the doctrine of indulgences, the Pope can draw upon the treasury of supererogatory merits to supply the deficiencies of needy members. Through auricular confession, the priest obtains possession of the inmost secrets of individuals and families. In the case of disobedience, the Church imposes severe penalties; and where it is free to use external force, it resorts at last to the stake. With such a system, it is not strange that Roman ecclesiastics have almost unlimited power over their members. Resistance to priestly authority not only subjects the laity to temporal persecution, but it also cuts them off, as they are taught to believe, from the hope of eternal life.

In the light of the foregoing statement of facts and principles, we are better prepared to consider a number of points relating directly or indirectly to popular education, especially in this country.

1. The idea of temporal power is inherent in the Ultramontane conception of the Papacy. As the rep-

resentative of God in the world, the Pope is logically the source of all authority, whether ecclesiastical or secular. Civil rulers are bound to obey him. In the famous bull, *Unam sanctam*, of Boniface VIII., it is declared that "The spiritual sword is to be used by the Church, but the carnal sword for the Church. The one in the hands of the priest, the other in the hands of kings and soldiers, but at the will and pleasure of the priest. It is right that the temporal sword and authority be subject to the spiritual power. . . . Moreover, we declare, say, define, and pronounce, that every human being should be subject to the Roman pontiff." The Papacy at the present day has not receded from its claims during the Middle Ages. The papal "Syllabus of Errors" of 1864, which must now be regarded as an infallible and irreformable declaration of principles, condemns the following propositions: "24. The Church has not the power of availing herself of force, or any direct or indirect temporal power . . . 27. The ministers of the Church and the Roman pontiff ought to be absolutely excluded from all charge and dominion over temporal affairs. . . 42. In the case of conflicting laws between the two powers, the civil law ought to prevail." In this same Syllabus it is declared that the Church is absolutely independent of the State in the exercise of authority; that the obligations of Catholic teachers and authors are not confined to dogmas of faith; that Roman pontiffs have never exceeded the limits of their power; that the Church has the innate and legitimate right of acquisition and possession; and that the immunity of the Church and of ecclesiastical persons is not derived from the civil law. In these statements the Papacy shows itself to-day what it has been in the past; it disowns no part of its history, and reaffirms the preposterous claims of the Middle Ages. It is a mistake to suppose that the Papacy has been influenced in its essential principles by modern progress. Lulled by this belief, we have become somewhat indifferent to the schemes and efforts of its representatives. In the "Syllabus of Errors" already referred to, the proposition is explicitly condemned that "the Roman pontiff can and ought to reconcile himself to and agree with progress, liberalism, and civilization, as lately introduced." By this declaration the Pope shows himself out of sympathy with modern civilization, and opposed to its broad and tolerant spirit. He places himself at the head of a reactionary body, that seeks to set up again the despotic reign of the dark ages.

2. The Papacy specifically repudiates religious freedom. This is consistent with its fundamental claim.

As the infallible source of all religious truth, it is necessarily intolerant. The Syllabus condemns the two following propositions: "77. In the present day, it is no longer expedient that the Catholic religion shall be held as the only religion of the State, to the exclusion of all other modes of worship. 78. Whence it has been wisely provided by law, in some countries called Catholic, that persons coming to reside therein shall enjoy the public exercise of their own worship." The desire and aim of the Papacy is to establish the Roman Catholic religion in every country, to exclude every other form of worship and belief, and if necessary to impose its faith by force upon all men. The Syllabus denies that "Every man is free to embrace and profess the religion he shall believe true, guided by the light of reason." Religious liberty is tolerated by the Papacy only where it can not be successfully resisted.

The Papacy has not relaxed in its bitterness toward Protestantism. Protestants are declared to be exposed to the pains of eternal damnation, and every prelate is sworn to oppose them. The papal bull *In Coena Domini* clearly sets forth the attitude of the Roman See toward heretics and infringers of its privileges. This bull was formerly read every year at Easter time, but in 1770, though its principles are still binding on the Papacy, its annual promulgation was discontinued from considerations of expediency. "In the name of God Almighty, Father, Son, and Holy Ghost, and by the authority of the blessed apostles, Peter and Paul, and by our own, we excommunicate and anathematize all Hussites, Wyclifites, Lutherans, Zwinglians, Calvinists, Huguenots, Anabaptists, and other apostates from the faith; and all other heretics, by whatsoever name they are called or of whatsoever sect they may be. And also their adherents, receivers, favorers, and generally any defenders of them; with all who, without our authority or that of the Apostolic See, knowingly read or retain, or in any way or from any cause, publicly or privately, or from any pretext, defend their books containing heresy or treating of religion; as also schismatics, and those who withdraw themselves, or recede obstinately from their obedience to us or the existing Roman pontiff." *The Rambler*, a Catholic paper of London, is merely consistent and outspoken in the following extract: "Religious liberty, in the sense of a liberty possessed by every man to choose his religion, is one of the most wicked delusions ever foisted upon this age by the father of all deceit. The very name of liberty—except in the sense of a permission to do certain definite acts—ought to be banished from the domain of religion. It is neither more nor less than a falsehood. *No man has a right to choose his religion.* None but an atheist can uphold the principles of religious liberty. Shall I foster that damnable doctrine that Socinianism, and Calvinism, and Anglicanism, and Judaism, are not every one of them mortal sins, like murder and adultery? Shall I hold out hopes to my erring Protestant brother that I will not meddle with his creed if he will not meddle with mine? Shall I tempt him to forget that he has no more right to his religious views than he has to my purse, to my house, or to my life-blood? No, Catholicism is the most intolerant of creeds. It is intolerance itself; for it is truth itself."* Roman Catholics in this country have predicted that men now living would see the majority of the people of the United States papists; that Catholicism is destined to become the State religion; and that plans are in operation for gaining a complete victory over Protestantism.

3. The Papacy does not tolerate intellectual freedom. In his function as universal teacher, the Pope claims authority over the intellects of men. In an allocution condemning the Christian League, an organization for the circulation of the Scriptures in Italy, Gregory XVI. speaks as follows: "Accordingly it is your duty to remove from the hands of the faithful

---
* Our Country, p. 48.

Bibles translated into the vulgar tongue, such as have been published contrary to the decrees of the Roman pontiffs, and all other prohibited or dangerous books, and to see that the faithful themselves by your admonitions and authority *may learn what kind of food they should consider wholesome, and what noxious and deadly.*"

In an allocution in 1862, Pius IX. urges the same duty still more vigorously. "You know, in short, that whatever is of the last importance is at stake when there is a question of our most holy belief of the Catholic Church. . . . Thus, as much as in you lies, apply yourselves to withdrawing the faithful from the contagion of so terrible a scourge; remove from their hands and from their sight wicked books and journals; impress on their hearts assiduously the precepts of our august religion; instruct them, warn them, exhort them to fly from those teachers of iniquity as they would fly from the presence of a serpent."*

The contagion referred to, which is to be shunned as "the presence of a serpent," is Protestant literature. The text-books in Roman Catholic schools are mutilated and falsified in the interests of Rome. In Fredet's "Modern History," for example, we find the following in reference to the Massacre of St. Bartholomew:

---

* De Montor, Roman Pontiffs, Vol. II.

"It is certain that religion had nothing to do with the massacre. . . . The only share which bishops, priests, and monks took in it was to save as many as they could of the Protestants. . . . It is objected that Pope Gregory XIII. publicly returned thanks to God on that occasion; but . . . the Pope rejoiced for the preservation of the French monarch and his kingdom." The prohibitory catalogue of the Papacy includes the ablest works of modern times in leading departments of learning. In it we find such names as Hallam, Hume, Gibbon, Mosheim, Sismondi, Ranke, Kant, Locke, Bacon, Des Cartes, Whately, Cousin, Montesquieu, Milton, and the Reformers. In the interests of its domination, the Papacy undertakes to keep the mind in bondage, to prevent free investigation, and to shut out the light. The Bible is practically prohibited. The Council of Trent passed ten rules in relation to prohibited books, which rules were approved by Pius IV. in a bull issued in 1564. The fourth rule is as follows: "Inasmuch as it is manifest from experience, that if the Holy Bible, translated into the vulgar tongue, be indiscriminately allowed to every one, the temerity of men will cause more evil than good to arise from it, it is, on this point, referred to the judgment of the bishops or inquisitors, who may, by the advice of the priest or confessor, permit the reading of the Bible translated into the vulgar tongue by Catholic authors, to those persons whose faith and piety, they apprehend, will be augmented, and not injured by it; and this permission they must have in writing. But if any one shall have the presumpton to read or possess it without such written permission, he shall not receive absolution until he have first delivered up such Bible to the ordinary. Booksellers, however, who shall sell, or otherwise dispose of Bibles in the vulgar tongue, to any person not having such permission, shall forfeit the value of the books, to be applied by the bishop to some pious use, and be subjected by the bishop to such other penalties as the bishop shall judge proper, according to the quality of the offense."*

4. It forms an important part of the papal scheme to have control of the young. To let the children of the Church grow up out of the circle of its influence, to imbibe instruction from prohibited books and heretical teachers, to hear history impartially discussed, would be dangerous to papal supremacy. At all hazards, therefore, the Papacy is bound to keep control of the education of its children. It denies the right of the State to take charge of education. The Syllabus already quoted, condemns the following propositions:

---
*Smets, Concilii Tridentini.

"47. The best theory of civil society requires that popular schools open to children of all classes and, generally, all public institutes intended for instruction in letters and philosophy, and for conducting the education of the young, should be freed from all ecclesiastical authority, government, and interference, and should be fully subject to the civil and political power, in conformity with the will of rulers and the prevalent opinions of the age. 48. The system of instructing youth, which consists in separating it from the Catholic faith and from the power of the Church, and in teaching exclusively, or at least primarily, the knowledge of natural things and the earthly ends of social life alone, may be approved by Catholics." The feeling and purpose of the Papacy are here clearly indicated. Religious instruction, by which is meant a training in the peculiar doctrines of Romanism, is to be the basis or principal element in education. The schools are to be under ecclesiastical jurisdiction, which includes the selection of text-books and the appointment of teachers. In the presence of this overriding claim, the State has nothing to do with the education of its future citizens.

The attitude of the Papacy towards our public school system was clearly and forcibly presented by the Rev. F. T. McCarthy, S. J., in a lecture delivered in Boston in December, 1887. He stated emphatically that he was not giving his individual opinion, but that of the Roman Catholic Church—a fact that is evident not only from the "Syllabus of Errors," but also from the fundamental principles of the Papacy. "The State," said Mr. McCarthy, "has no right to teach, no right to educate. When the State steps in and assumes the work of the teacher, then there is the invasion of the individual rights, of the domestic rights, of the rights of the Church, and of divine rights. There are no circumstances under which the State is allowed to teach. The Catholic Church teaches that if Catholics have other schools to send their children to, where they can receive a fitting education, and they send their children to godless schools, . . . they are guilty of mortal sin. We cannot allow this state of things [the public school system] to go on, without imperilling the salvation of your children and your own salvation." The Papacy is at open war with the public schools of our country.

The policy adopted by the Church is very simple. The third Plenary Council of American bishops, held in Baltimore in 1884, outlined it as follows: "Two objects then, dear brethren, we have in view: to multiply our schools, and to perfect them. We must multiply them till every Catholic child in the land shall have within its reach the means of education . . . Pastors and parents should not rest till this defect be remedied. No parish is complete till it have schools adequate to the needs of its children, and the pastor and people of such a parish should feel that they have not accomplished their entire duty until this want is supplied." Active steps are being taken to carry out this policy. The priest who has the ability to establish such a school, and yet fails to do it, thereby gives sufficient ground for his removal.

The principal means employed in undermining our school system is the Roman Catholic vote. There were in the United States in 1883 seventy-two Roman bishops, 6,546 priests, and 6,832,000 laymen. Not only in ecclesiastical, but also in political matters, they are obedient to the Pope. This is a tremendous power to rest in the hands of a shrewd and aggressive foreigner; and as recent events show, it is being skilfully used to build up the Roman Church. Votes are traded for favors and money. In the days of the notorious Tweed, several hundred thousand dollars were appropriated to the support of Catholic parochial schools in New York. There are at present large Roman Catholic institutions in New York City—the House of the Sisters of Mercy in 81st street, the Foundling Asylum of the Sisters of Charity in 68th street, and the Catholic Protectory in Westchester—that are supported by the city treasury at a yearly expense of more than half a million dollars. The two former institutions are built upon blocks of ground worth hundreds of thousands of dollars each, that were given by the city through the favor of the Tammany ring.* These gifts were made in payment for political influence. "The authorities of New York City," says the Rev. Dr. Strong in "Our Country," "during the eleven years preceding 1880, gave the Roman Church real estate valued at $3,500,000, and money to the amount of $5,827,471; this in exchange for Romish votes, and every cent of it paid in violation of law." This illustrates the papal method. The same bargaining is going on in other cities; and in Poughkeepsie and New Haven a division of the public school fund has been secured.

5. Yet the Papacy is not favorable to the education of the masses. It seeks above all things absolute obedience on the part of its adherents. Intelligence among the laity is recognized as a dangerous possession; for it ministers to their independence in thinking, and makes them more critical of the teaching imposed upon them by priestly authority. Any activity displayed by the Papacy in popular education is forced by

---

*The New Know-Nothingism and the Old, by the Rev. Dr. McGlynn, in North American Review, August, 1887.

the existence of Protestant schools. The establishment of parish schools giving an education worth the name, is a measure of self-defense. The Jesuits, with all their lauded activity in education, never had the intellectual elevation of the masses at heart. With them education was a means of combating Protestantism, and of begetting a bigoted attachment to the Roman Church. Wherever the Papacy has had full control of education, the masses have been brought up in ignorance. It is a Jesuit maxim that "A few should be well educated; the people should be led. Reading and writing are enough for them." When Victor Emmanuel took possession of the Papal States in 1870, only five per cent. of the population could read and write. In thrift and intelligence Catholic countries do not compare favorably with Protestant countries. Macaulay's judgment on this point is as just as it is positive. "During the last three centuries, to stunt the growth of the human mind has been the chief object of the Church of Rome. Throughout Christendom, whatever advance has been made in knowlege, in freedom, in wealth, and in the arts of life, has been made in spite of her, and has everywhere been in inverse proportion to her power. The loveliest and most fertile provinces of Europe have, under her rule, been sunk in poverty, in political servitude, and in intellectual torpor, while

Protestant countries, once proverbial for sterility and barbarism, have been turned by skill and industry into gardens, and can boast of a long list of heroes and statesmen, philosophers and poets."*

From the preceding discussion we may easily deduce the line of action that is necessary to protect our institutions, particularly our public school system, against papal aggression.

1. We should carefully observe the insidious movements of the Papacy.

2. Recognizing the separation of Church and State wisely made by the Constitution, we should nowhere tolerate sectarian legislation.

3. Maintaining the right of the State to educate its citizens, we should forbid the appropriation of any public funds to sectarian schools.

4. All public school offices should be filled with recognized friends of popular education.

5. The rights of conscience should be maintained and defended by the State.

---

*History of England, Chap. I., where the striking contrast between Protestant and Roman Catholic countries is graphically presented.

CHAPTER III.

PROTESTANTISM AND POPULAR EDUCATION.

THE word Protestant originated under circumstances that formed a crisis in history. At the imperial Diet of Spires in 1529, the Roman Catholic party succeeded in passing a decree that restored the celebration of the mass wherever it had been abolished, excluded from the pulpit every preacher that did not recognize transubstantiation in the sacrament, established a rigid censorship of books, and forbade any effort to promulgate the principles of the Reformation. The execution of the decree would have brought the reformatory movement to a speedy termination. Against this decree, which had the sanction of the Pope and of the emperor Charles V., the evangelical princes at the Diet drew up a formal *protest* in which they said: "We are resolved, with the grace of God, to maintain the pure and exclusive preaching of his only Word, such as it is contained in the biblical books of the Old and New Testament, without adding anything thereto that may be contrary to it. This Word is the only truth; it is the sure rule of all doctrine and of all life, and can never fail nor deceive us. He who builds on this foundation shall stand against all the powers of hell, while all the human vanities that are set up against it shall fall before the face of God." This protest, from which the appellation Protestant is derived, involves, as we shall see, principles of deep significance.

The same principles were announced at an earlier date, under circumstances no less important and imposing. In 1521 Luther was summoned before the imperial Diet of Worms to answer the charge of heresy. It was a magnificent assembly presided over by Charles V. himself. Luther acknowleged himself the author of a number of books, the titles of which had been read. "You are required," said the speaker of the Diet, "to give a clear and precise answer. Will you, or will you not, retract?" The great Reformer replied: "Since your imperial Majesty and your highnesses ask me for a short and plain answer, I will give you one without horns or teeth. Except I can be convinced by Holy Scripture, or by clear and indisputable reasons from other sources (for I cannot defer simply to the Pope or to Councils, since it is clear that they have often erred), I neither can nor will retract anything. As it has been found impossible to refute the proofs I have quoted, my conscience is a prisoner to God's Word; and no one can be compelled to act against his conscience. Here I stand; I can not do otherwise. God help me, Amen!" In this declaration, as in the protest at the Diet of Spires, the principle of secular and ecclesiastical authority in matters of faith is rejected. The appeal is made from the Pope and the emperor to the Word of God, or to clear and convincing reason. With his conscience enlightened by Holy Scripture, the individual man asserts his spiritual independence, and his immediate responsibility to God alone.

The principle of personal liberty, as announced by Luther and the other leading Reformers, has been misunderstood. It has been charged by papal writers that the word Protestant signifies resistance to the emperor and the Pope, or to all lawfully constituted authority. Nothing could be farther from the truth. Luther and his coadjutors simply returned to the scriptural principle that in matters of faith we should obey God rather than man. The protest at Spires was not against authority, but against a usurpation of authority that undertook to tyrannize over the Christian conscience. The principle of the Reformers was not absolute liberty to do as we please—a doctrine that issues in social and ecclesiastical anarchy; it was freedom to obey the dictates of a conscience illumined by the Word of God. This freedom, instead of leading to confusion, conduces to order. The Scriptures become its law; and in accordance with their teaching, every evil passion is restrained; honor is rendered to every rightly constituted authority; and discord is banished by brotherly love.

In the Protestant creeds that resulted from the Reformation we find, along with many points of substantial agreement, a number of articles directly opposed to the distinctive tenets of the Romish faith. All the points of difference, however, may be reduced to three comprehensive and fundamental principles, the wide-reaching significance of which can hardly be exaggerated. They are the fundamental principles of Protestantism, and may be stated as follows: 1. The Holy Scriptures of the Old and the New Testament are the only rule of faith and practice in matters of religion. 2. Man is justified by faith alone; and 3. All believers become kings and priests unto God. These principles, when taken in their full significance, will be found to provide a firm basis and lasting impulse for popular education.

I. *The Scriptures as Rule of Faith.*—In the "Book of Concord," composed of the different Lutheran confessional writings, it is said: "The Holy Scriptures alone remain the only judge, rule, and standard, according to which, as the only test-stone, all dogmas should and must be discerned and judged, as to whether they be good or evil, right or wrong." The "Thirty-nine Articles" of the Church of England say: "Holy Scripture containeth all things necessary to salvation; so that whatsoever is not read therein, nor may be proved thereby, is not to be required of any man, that it should be believed as an article of the Faith, or be thought requisite or necessary to salvation." The Bible was the weapon that the Reformers used against the Papacy. By it they judged papal traditions, and the decrees of Councils. In its light they discovered and condemned errors in the Roman Church; and before its tribunal they summoned the Pope himself. In a word, they were able to restore to the world the Christianity of the New Testament, and to justify the name of *evangelical* which they assumed.

The conception of the Church was changed. It was held to be the body of true believers, who are united by faith to Christ as the head. The supremacy of the Pope was rejected and his infallibility denied. The sacrifice of the mass was discarded because it is said in Heb. x. 10 (and elsewhere substantially), that "We are sanctified through the offering of the body of Christ once for all." Preaching as the divinely appointed means of public instruction in religious truth, was made prominent as in the Apostolic Church. The celibacy of the clergy was rejected not only because of the scandal attending it, but also because, as the Augsburg Confession says, "No law of man, no vow, can take away the commandment of God and his ordinance." The spiritual and secular powers, in opposition to the preposterous claims of the Papacy, were distinctly separated. Both powers were instituted of God, and each in its sphere should be respected and honored. The ecclesiastical power was expressly forbidden to interfere with secular government.* If the Protestant countries of Europe placed the secular power over the Church, their action resulted, not from their primary principles, but from the necessities of the times. The interposition of the secular authority was necessary to give unity to the Protestant movement. In America Protestant principles have found their full expression in the complete separation of Church and State. Each is recognized as of divine origin, but with different functions; and while they exist side by side in harmony, neither trespasses on the sphere of the other.

II. *Justification by Faith.*—Luther attached great importance to this doctrine as the central truth of the

---

* Augsburg Confession, Art. XXVIII.

Reformation. In the Smalcald Articles he says: "We must be sure concerning this doctrine, and not doubt; for otherwise all is lost, and the Pope and the devil and all things against us gain the victory."

The Reformation worked itself out in Luther before he gave its principles to the world. In his religious experience, the truth of justification by faith stands pre-eminent. Though in the convent at Erfurt he had rigidly conformed to all the requirements of the Roman Church, he had not been able to find perfect peace. The consciousness of sin weighed upon his mind, and Christ was dreaded as an exacting judge. He longed for sweet communion with God. In 1511 he went to Rome on a mission for the Augustinian brotherhood. For the sake of obtaining an indulgence promised by the Pope, he began one day to climb Pilate's staircase on his knees. While performing this supposed meritorious act, the declaration of the Scriptures (which he had long been studying) suddenly broke upon his mind in full-orbed splendor, "The just shall live by faith." He arose at once from his knees; and in his joy, as he tells us, he "felt like a new man, and entered through the open doors into the very paradise of God."

While the Roman system interposes a mediating priesthood between God and man, and makes the assurance of salvation an official communication, the Protestant doctrine of justification brings the soul into immediate relation with God. Through the Gospel, the heart is opened to believe and love God; there is a consciousness of the forgiveness of sin; there is a new joy in the restoration of the soul to its Creator; and there is a satisfying of all the deepest needs and longings of the religious nature. In this transforming experience the Christian finds his assurance. The Gospel is no longer an external matter; it has been embodied in his thought and feeling. As a result, a Christian consciousness has been formed. It is this consciousness that gives the necessary qualifications to interpret the Scriptures in their deepest significance. It does not need an infallible ecclesiastic to authorize an interpretation. The soul has been brought into harmony with the Gospel; it has become the abode of the Holy Spirit; it immediately discerns and appropriates the truth according to its needs.

III. *The Priesthood of Believers.*—As we have seen, the Reformers taught that by faith we have immediate access to God. Needing the intervention of no special sacerdotal class, such as existed under the Papacy or the Jewish dispensation, all Christians have now the privileges that once pertained to the hierarchical office. They approach trustfully into the presence of God; they offer him the incense of praise and thanksgiving; they intercede for themselves and all mankind. In his treatise "On Christian Liberty," Luther presents this truth very forcibly: "Nor are we only kings and the freest of all men, but also priests forever, a dignity far higher than kingship, because by that priesthood we are worthy to appear before God, to pray for others, and to teach one another mutually the things which are of God. For these are the duties of priests, and they can not possibly be permitted to any unbeliever. Christ has obtained for us this favor, if we believe in Him, that, just as we are his brethren and co-heirs and fellow-kings with Him, so we should be also fellow-priests with Him, and venture with confidence, through the spirit of faith, to come into the presence of God, and cry 'Abba, Father!' and to pray for one another, and to do all things which we see done and figured in the visible and corporal office of priesthood."

This doctrine of the universal priesthood of believers bestows upon them great honor. At one blow it breaks the bondage of the laity as it exists under the Papacy. They are bound in their religious life by no external human authority. They are freemen in Christ. In this independent position, life is dignified by the weight of grave responsibilities. Every one must watch over his own religious faith and practice. While giving due honor to their religious teachers, Christians are not bound to an unquestioning submission, but test all instruction by the Word of God.

The three fundamental principles of Protestantism, which we have been considering, necessitate and encourage popular education in various ways.

1. The Bible is placed in the hands of the laity. It is looked upon not as a volume unsafe because of its obscurities, but as a treasure invaluable because of its divine message. Yet it is not violently severed from the teaching of the Church in past ages. The Reformation did not give to the world what was absolutely new; it was essentially a restoration of truth that had long been obscured or forgotten. With the Scriptures as guide the Reformers traversed the preceding centuries and sought out an evangelical Christianity. The three œcumenical creeds were incorporated in the Protestant confessions of faith; and wherever the Church fathers were found to be evangelical, they were gladly quoted as authorities.

This use of the Bible as the ultimate source of religious truth rendered general education a necessity—a fact that has been clearly and forcibly presented by a distinguished French scholar: "In rendering man responsible for his faith, and in placing the source of that faith in Holy Scripture, the Reformation contracted the obligation of placing every one in a condition to save himself by reading and studying the Bible. Instruction became then the first of the duties of charity; and all who had charge of souls, from the father of a family to the magistrates of cities and to the sovereign of the State, were called upon, in the name of their own salvation, and each according to the measure of his responsibility, to favor popular education. Thus Protestantism . . . placed in the service of education the most effective stimulus and the most powerful interest that can be brought to bear upon men."*

The Bible itself, both as a religious manual and as a literary work, is a potent instrument of culture. No other book is half so useful in leading man towards his goal as a moral and religious being. It surrounds life with an atmosphere of purity, love, and truth. It gives comfort in sorrow; cheers with precious promises; ministers strength in hours of weakness and temptation; restrains evil tendencies; fills our social relations with affection; explains the universe; and unites us to God. As Burns has beautifully shown in his "Cotter's Saturday Night," it glorifies a humble, laboring life. From a literary point of view the Bible

---

* Michel Bréal, Quelques Mots sur l' Instruction Publique en France.

is a remarkable book. Nearly every department of literature is represented in its pages. It contains the most important of all history. Without its opening chapters—interpret them as we may—what a riddle the world and human life would be! In the story of the Chosen People we see the hand of God at work in history. The civil regulations of the ancient Jews are models of wisdom and justice. Abraham, Moses, David, and Paul are heroes, whose lives are grand in faith, wisdom, and achievement. In Proverbs and Ecclesiastes there is a great store of practical truth. In the Psalms and the Prophets we find not only the finest religious poetry in all literature, but also many passages of astonishing eloquence and power. Let the Bible in its moral, religious, and literary character be taken into the life of a man, and the result is a great uplifting in culture.

2. The duties of secular government and of all social relations have the stigma of worldliness taken away. The statements of the sixteenth article of the Augsburg Confession are remarkable: "Concerning civil affairs, they teach that such civil ordinances as are lawful, are good works of God; that Christians may lawfully bear civil office, sit in judgments, determine matters by the imperial laws and other laws in present force, appoint just punishments, engage in just

war, act as soldiers, make legal bargains and contracts, hold property, take an oath when magistrates require it, marry a wife, or be given in marriage. . . . . They condemn also those that place the perfection of the Gospel, not in the fear of God, and in faith, but in forsaking civil offices, inasmuch as the Gospel teacheth an everlasting righteousness of the heart."

The principles of Protestantism do not unduly depreciate the present life in the interests of the life to come. Our mission here is not to fast, to make pilgrimages, and to withdraw into monasteries, but faithfully to perform the duties that come to us in every relation of life. Religion is not a thing apart from our daily labors, but a spirit sanctifying our whole life, and ennobling the lowliest service. Domestic institutions are highly honored as the divine ideal. Luther speaks often and tenderly of the marriage relation; and with his beloved Catharine, he established a model home, filled with affection and happiness.

To fulfil the duties of this rich human life, as contemplated by Protestantism, intelligence is necessary. No class should be left in ignorance. Education is an interest of the State no less than of the Church. Its aim should be to fit the young for useful living in every relation. "Even if there were no soul," says

Luther, "and men did not need schools and the languages for the sake of Christianity and the Scriptures, still, for the establishment of the best schools everywhere, both for boys and girls, this consideration is of itself sufficient, namely, that society, for the maintenance of civil order and the proper regulation of the household, needs accomplished and well-trained men and women. Now such men are to come from boys, and such women from girls; hence it is necessary that boys and girls be properly taught and brought up."*
And again: "I maintain that the civil authorities are under obligation to compel the people to send their children to school. . . If the government can compel such citizens as are fit for military service to bear spear and rifle, to mount ramparts, and perform other martial duties in time of war; how much more has it a right to compel the people to send their children to school, because in this case we are warring with the devil, whose object it is secretly to exhaust our cities and principalities of their strong men, to destroy the kernel and leave a shell of ignorant and helpless people, whom he can sport and juggle with at pleasure."†

3. In Protestantism, Nature is restored to its rights. Under Romanism, which unduly magnifies a system of

---

* Address to the Mayors and Aldermen of the German Cities.
† Sermon on the Duty of Sending Children to School.

dogmas, and inculcates a one-sided religious life, the physical universe is depreciated. Protestantism looks upon the present world as a field for serving God in the exercise of our native powers and in the discharge of our natural duties. The wondrous beauty of nature is appreciated. Its phenomena are studied; and the knowledge thus acquired is turned to account in the service of man. It is not an accident that the leaders of modern science have come from Protestant countries. Protestantism encourages investigation, welcomes discoveries, applies new ideas, and favors progress. Luther was justified in saying, "We are at the dawn of a new era, for we are beginning to recover the knowlege of the external world that we had lost since the fall of Adam... We already recognize in the most delicate flower the wonders of divine goodness and the omnipotence of God." The barrenness of exclusively linguistic studies has been relieved by studies treating of various departments of Nature. The gain in this particular has been great. But a leading benefit is the new basis upon which education itself has been placed. A true science of education has been established, the principles of which are found, not in some theological tenet, but in human nature. The effort is made to develop the native physical, mental, and moral powers in the direction of a perfect manhood. The repressive and cruel discipline of the Middle Ages has given place to a fostering and gentle training. The school-room is made attractive, and study pleasant; the natural activity of children is utilized, and their innate desire for knowlege is gratified. To use the strong language of Luther in the address already quoted, "Our schools are no longer a hell and purgatory, in which children are tortured over cases and tenses, and in which with much flogging, trembling, anguish, and wretchedness, they learn nothing."

4. Influenced by their fundamental principles, the Reformers early began to labor for the establishment and improvement of schools. As early as 1524 Luther made an appeal of marvelous energy to the authorities of the German cities in behalf of popular education. If we consider its pioneer character, in connection with its statement of principles, we must regard the address as the most important educational treatise ever written. Education remained through Luther's whole life a cherished interest, and he has treated of it in many sermons and letters. There is scarcely any phase of the subject that he did not touch upon, and everywhere he exhibited masterly penetration and judgment. "If we survey the pedagogy of Luther in all its extent," says a distinguished German educator, "and imagine it fully realized in

practice, what a splendid picture the schools and education of the sixteenth century would present! We should have courses of study, text-books, teachers, methods, principles, and modes of discipline, schools and school regulations, that could serve as models for our own age."* The great need Luther saw during the visitation of the churches of Saxony led him in 1529 to prepare his two catechisms for the instruction of the clergy and the laity. In 1534 he published his translation of the Bible, which had an extraordinary educational influence upon Germany. By his repeated appeals in behalf of education, all Protestant Germany was aroused. In 1525 he was commissioned by the Duke of Mansfield to establish two schools in his native town Eisleben, one for primary and the other for secondary instruction. Both in the courses of study and in the methods of instruction, these schools served as models for many others. The forms of church government adopted by the various Protestant states and cities contain provisions for the establishment and management of schools. The "Saxony School Plan," originally prepared by Melancthon and revised by Luther in 1538, was extensively adopted. The current abuses of the schools in studies and discipline were pointed out. "In order

---

* Dittes, Geschichte der Erziehung und des Unterrichts.

that the young may be properly taught," says the Plan, "we have established this form:

"1. The teachers shall see to it that the children are taught only Latin, not German or Hebrew as some have hitherto done, who have burdened their pupils with too many studies, which are not only useless but hurtful. . . .

"2. They shall not burden the children with many books, but in every way avoid a distracting multiplicity of studies.

"3. It is necessary that the children be divided into grades."

Except the neglect of the mother-tongue, the whole Plan, which extends to minute details, is admirable. In a few years the Protestant portion of Germany had greatly increased the number of schools, which, though defective in many particulars, were far superior to any that had previously existed. Melanchthon, Zwingli, Calvin, were all active in educational work.

Protestant nations were the first to establish a system of public schools. Catholic nations imitated them only under the stress of political necessity, and then in opposition to papal teaching, which makes education an exclusive function of the Church. The countries at present most distinguished for intelligence and freedom are Protestant. In so far as any nation, as

France, Austria, or Italy, has freed itself from Ultramontane domination, it has bestowed greater care upon the instruction of the people, and removed the stigma of illiteracy. When the Papacy, under the shock of the Reformation, began as a measure of self-defence to exercise more rigidly its repressive authority over the intellect of its adherents, Catholic nations gradually fell behind in the march of progress. At the opening of the sixteenth century, Italy was the centre of the new culture resulting from the revival of learning. A few decades later, Spain exhibited a brief period of literary bloom. But the strict censorship established by the Papacy and exercised through the Inquisition proved fatal to literary activity; and in the last three hundred years, as the result of their servile condition, Italy and Spain have produced scarcely a writer of international repute. The Augustan age of French literature under Louis XIV. is not to be attributed to the Papacy. Under the leadership of Bossuet the moderate Gallican type of Romanism was in the ascendency. The brilliant court of the king was the centre and stimulus of culture; and literature flourished, not because of Ultramontane Rome, but in spite of it. The case is different with Protestant nations. Their history exhibits progress in intelligence, prosperity, and freedom. After the Reformation the centre of culture moved northward; and the superiority of Protestant training was magnificently attested on the fields of Sadowa and Sedan, and in the ascendency of Prussia. The universities of northern Germany are foremost in learning. In England the brilliant era of Elizabeth was largely due to the literary activity and intellectual freedom brought about by the Reformation. In America, while Mexico has been weighed down by illiteracy and superstition, the United States have achieved distinction for the intelligence, freedom, and welfare of the people. The foundation of this remarkable progress was laid by the Puritans in 1647, when the General Court of the Massachusetts colony passed the following order: "It being one chief object of the old deluder Satan to keep men from the knowledge of the Scriptures, as in former times by keeping them in an unknown tongue, so in these latter times by persuading from the use of tongues, that so at least the true sense and meaning of the original might be clouded by false glosses of saint-seeming deceivers; that learning may not be buried in the grave of our fathers in the Church and Commonwealth, the Lord assisting our endeavors, it is therefore *ordered*, that every township in this jurisdiction, after the Lord hath increased them to the number of fifty householders, shall then forthwith appoint one within their town to teach all such children as shall resort to him to write and read, &c.* Other colonies followed the example of Massachusetts; and thus the popular education of this country sprang directly from Protestant principles.

5. The principles of Protestantism concern man as an individual. This is their starting point. In harmony with the Gospel, they place man in an independent position, and dignify him with the responsibility of ascertaining and performing his duty immediately in the sight of God. The ideal of life is a faithful discharge of every duty, both private and public, in the fear of God. Inasmuch as this ideal cannot be attained without intelligence, instruction becomes a necessity to the individual, and a duty to those entrusted with the care of youth. It is different under Romanism, where the Church is the supreme object of concern. The supremacy of the Church—a thought lying at the basis of Roman Catholic education—is the chief factor in determining subjects of study and methods of instruction. According to the Catholic view, the principal end of education is, not to develop the native powers in the direction of an ideal manhood, but to make faithful and obedient members of the Church or subjects of the Pope. "The Catholic view does not recognize the individ-

---

*Painter, History of Education, p. 312.

ual's right to Christian education and instruction, and therefore it feels no obligation to provide for the culture of all its members. The Church is the supreme object of life, and therefore, of culture; the school and the home are hence only means to bring up the young for obedience and service in the Church. The individual is an object of ecclesiastical activity only so far as the Church has an interest in him for her own ends. This is indeed the strength and weakness of the Catholic system; this the secret of Catholic pedagogy before and since the Reformation—that every thing is a means for that one end; the science that she encourages and teaches, and the ignorance she fosters and promotes, faith and superstition, culture and barbarism, the severest discipline that she exercises as well as the license that she tolerates,—*omnia in majorem Dei, i. e. ecclesiæ, gloriam.* To this ecclesiastical Christianity the evangelical Christianity of the Reformation is opposed. Here the aim and end of all the activity of the Church is not the institution but *the person*, not the system but *the man;* not the glory of the external Church, but the salvation of the individual soul. The Reformation wishes nothing else than what Christianity itself wishes—*that all be helped, that all come to the knowledge of the truth.* Thus, at every point of the Protestant system of education, appears the endless worth of personality, but therewith the endless rights, as well as the endless obligations and responsibilities, of the human soul. As such every man has a right to be instructed in faith, to be brought up in Christian doctrine and life, and thereby be placed in a position to edify himself from the Word of God, and to become that which every man should become according to the purpose of God—a child of God, a citizen of the kingdom of God, an heir of life. But to this end he needs the education of his will, the awakening of his understanding, and the communication of that knowledge which is necessary for a fruitful hearing, reading, comprehension, and right application of the divine Word. Thus follows, from the Protestant doctrine of salvation, the right of every man to Christian education and instruction, and the corresponding duty of the Christian community to make the necessary provision therefor."*

In view of this discussion, it clearly appears that in principle and in fact Protestantism is the mother of popular education and the friend of culture.

---

* Schmid, Pedagog. Handbuch.

CHAPTER IV.

EDUCATION BEFORE THE REFORMATION.

FOR nearly a thousand years after the downfall of Rome in 476, the ascetic spirit in religion, which George Eliot has strikingly characterized as "otherworldliness," exerted a powerful influence in Europe. It manifested itself in various forms of self-abnegation; hermits withdrew into the wilderness to live in squalor, and monks shut themselves up in monasteries under the vows of poverty, chastity, and obedience. This ascetic tendency was a natural reaction against the sensuousness of heathenism. When the Church came to assert itself in opposition to heathen life, it gave undue prominence to our spiritual interests. Science was sunk in theology, and education was stamped with a theological character that fettered it for ages.

In studying the Middle Ages, we need to be on our guard against magnifying their defects. The dark ages should not be made too dark. While ignorance prevailed in large measure, it was not universal. There is an education of the hand and will, as well as of the intellect; and it often happened that men who could not read, were able to lead armies and govern kingdoms. It was an age of action; a formative period for happier ages; a transitional era, in which Christianity and civilization were being communicated to the future standard-bearers of progress. It was the age of cathedrals —those miracles in stone; it saw the rise of great commercial centres, and of an influential middle class. The institution of chivalry brought forward ennobling ideals. Great modern languages assumed a literary character, and embodied a notable literature. In Germany we find an epic, the *Nibelungenlied*, that deserves to rank with the world's greatest masterpieces. A voluminous poetic literature was created. Scholars were not wanting; Abelard, Anselm, Aquinas, Duns Scotus, were men of acute understanding and large attainments. The universities were founded, and frequented by armies of students. These facts, in connection with numerous inventions and discoveries, are inconsistent with an age of absolute darkness. The educational institutions of the period will now be considered in succession.

1. *Monastic Schools.*—Under the impulse of asceticism, monasteries rapidly multiplied, and by the seventh century were scattered throughout all the countries of Europe. The Benedictine order in particular

became large and influential. As long as they remained uncorrupted by wealth and power, the monasteries were asylums for the oppressed; missionary stations for the conversion of the heathen; repositories of learning; the principal abodes of the arts and sciences.

As the heathen schools had now disappeared, the monasteries engaged in educational work. The Church regarded education as one of its exclusive functions, and under its direction nearly all instruction had an ecclesiastical character. The purely secular studies of the *trivium*—grammar, rhetoric, and dialectic—and of the *quadrivium*—music, arithmetic, geometry, and astronomy — were pursued chiefly in the interests of the Church. Latin, the language of the Church, was made the basis of instruction, to the well-nigh universal neglect of the mother-tongue. The works of the Church fathers were read, though expurgated editions of the Latin classics were used. Logic was applied to theology, arithmetic extended to only a few simple rules, geometry consisted in scanty extracts from Euclid, astronomy was limited in most schools to the arrangement of the Church calendar, and music was confined to learning hymns. The pedagogy of the ninth century may be judged by the following extract from Rhabanus Maurus: "Arithmetic is important on account of the secrets contained in the numbers; the Scriptures also encourage its study, since they speak of numbers and measures. Geometry is necessary, because in Scripture circles of all kinds occur in the building of the ark, and Solomon's temple. Music and astronomy are required in connection with divine service, which can not be celebrated with dignity and decency without music, nor on fixed and definite days without astronomy."

2. *Cathedral and Parochial Schools.*—Besides the convent or monastic schools, there were two other classes of schools that owed their origin to the Church during the Middle Ages—the cathedral and the parochial schools. The cathedral schools received their perfected organization in the eighth century. The priests connected with each cathedral Church were organized into a brotherhood, one of whose foremost duties was to establish and conduct schools. While these were designed chiefly for candidates for the priesthood, they were yet open to others. The instruction embraced the seven liberal arts, as they were called, of the *trivium* and *quadrivium*, but the religious element was made still more prominent than in the convent schools.

The parochial schools were established in the separate parishes, under the supervision of the priest.

They were designed to acquaint the young with the elements of Christian doctrine, to prepare them for intelligent participation in public worship, and especially to introduce them into Church membership. Reading and writing did not usually form any part of the course of study, and their function was similar to that of the catechetical schools of the early Church. But "the majority of the clergy," says Neander, "who came in immediate contact with the people, possessed no other qualification for their office than a certain skill and expertness in performing the ceremonies of the Church. The liturgical element would thus of necessity tend continually to acquire an undue predominance, suiting as it did the prevalent idea of the priesthood; while the didactic element—an element so important for promoting the religious knowledge which was so neglected among the people—would, on the other hand, retreat more and more into the background."

3. *Secular Education.*—Secular education, which came into prominence in the latter half of the Middle Ages, took two directions: chivalry gave rise to what may be called knightly education, and the cities to burgher education. These secular tendencies were in part a reaction against the one-sided religious character of the ecclesiastical schools, and in part the natural

product of peculiar social conditions. The despotic authority claimed by the hierarchy, in connection with its worldliness, excited distrust and resistance. The crusades, though at an almost incredible cost of life, contributed largely to the general advancement of Europe. The field of knowledge was widened, and commerce, trade, and manufacture were quickened. Coming at last to a feeling of self-consciousness and independence, the knightly and the burgher classes in a measure emancipated themselves from ecclesiastical tutelage.

Knightly education stood in sharp contrast with that of the Church. It attached importance to what the Church schools neglected and condemned. Physical culture received great attention; polished manners were carefully cultivated; and a love of glory was constantly instilled. Women were held in worshipful regard as the embodiment of virtue. The native tongue was cultivated and made the medium of all literary productions. Nature, instead of being placed in an unnatural opposition to spiritual interests, inspired the noblest sentiments and the purest joys. The chief intellectual elements in knightly culture were music and poetry; and one of the richest literary treasures coming down to us from the Middle Ages, is the large collection of knightly poetry comprehended under the term minne-songs.

With the growing importance of the commercial and artisan classes, there came the conscious need of an education adapted to the wants of practical life. Out of this need arose a class of schools which have borne different names, as town, burgher, or writing schools. In addition to reading, writing, and arithmetic, other practical studies—geography, history, and the mother-tongue—were pursued in a small way. Latin also was early introduced. Though the burgher schools were secular institutions in origin and aim, the clergy as the only authorized teachers claimed the right to control them. This claim, which was often resisted by the civil magistrates, gave rise to strife, in which sometimes the one party, and sometimes the other, was victorious. Where the civil authorities had control, they appointed laymen as teachers, whose duties were prescribed by a contract. The principal teacher, who was engaged for a year, employed and paid his assistants. The salaries barely sufficed to procure the necessaries of life.

Female education outside of the knightly order was generally neglected. Here and there in connection with nunneries a few women attained distinction by their learning, but these cases were exceptional. Among the knightly class, where women were held in high honor, great attention was paid to female culture. The young women were not only instructed in the feminine arts of sewing, knitting, embroidery, and house-keeping, but they were also given an intellectual training which in addition to reading, writing, and the mother-tongue, often included an extended acquaintance with Latin.

4. *The Universities.*—The awakened intellect of Europe manifested itself most strikingly toward the close of the Middle Ages in the founding of universities. They arose independently of both Church and State. In the beginning they consisted of free associations of learned men and aspiring youths, who were held together alone by their mutual interest in knowledge. In this way the University of Bologna had its origin in the twelfth century for the study of law, and the University of Salerno for the study of medicine. A few years after its establishment, the University of Bologna numbered no less than 12,000 students. In the twelfth century the cathedral school of Paris was enlarged into a university, and afterwards became the most celebrated seat of learning in Europe. At one time it was attended by more than 20,000 students, who for the purpose of better government were divided into separate bodies according to nationality. They had special halls called colleges, in which they lodged and boarded under official

supervision. The professors were divided into the four faculties of philosophy, theology, medicine, and law, which have since been retained in universities, though the studies in each department have been greatly enlarged.

Such were the various educational institutions in operation at the opening of the sixteenth century. Naturally sharing in the prevailing rudeness of the time, they were exceedingly defective in studies, methods, and discipline. The pupils were passive under instruction. The teachers lectured, dictated, interpreted, and the learners listened and memorized. The principle of authority prevailed. It was decided, for example, that there were no spots in the sun, because Aristotle had nowhere made mention of the fact. What seemed to be spots were therefore regarded as defects in the observer's glasses. There was but little intellectual freedom; the teachers were bound by the authority of Aristotle and the Church, and the pupils by the authority of the teacher. Education did not aim at a development of all the faculties, but at a storing of the memory with certain facts of more or less importance in relation to the Church or practical life. In the universities, obscure and often trifling questions in philosophy and theology engaged the attention.

The teachers corresponded in character to the meagre pay they received. Men not capable of making a living in any other way took to teaching. Though organized, according to the spirit of the time, in a guild, teachers commanded but little respect, and wandered from town to town in search of employment. There were no school houses, and in many places no organized schools. After coming to terms with the town authorities, these wandering teachers proceeded to gather about them a body of pupils. Without learning or pedagogical training, they were unqualified to conduct well-regulated schools. The discipline was severe, and often cruel. It was an age when authority depended largely on physical force; and servile submission was exacted from the pupil, and bodily chastisement was the ordinary means of correction. " Frequently at the installation of teachers a ferule was presented them as a mark of their dignity. Even with adults this sort of punishment was not without example. At the University of Paris as late as the fifteenth century the students were scourged on the naked back, and in the cloister of St. Gall it was the custom to bind offending monks to pillars, and after the removal of the outer garment to whip them. Even teachers, who were negligent in their office, had to submit to the same punishment."*

---

* Strack, Geschichte des deutschen Schulwesens.

The moral tone of the universities was low; brawls, outbreaks, and gross immorality were common.

There were, however, a few penetrating minds, especially in the latter part of the Middle Ages, that perceived and pointed out, in some measure, the existing defects in education. In their writings we find many a statement that would do credit to modern pedagogy. Anselm (born 1023), a distinguished theologian, did not wholly approve of the cruel discipline in vogue. "In educating youth," he said, "we should learn a lesson from artists, who do not fashion their gold and silver images with blows alone, but they press and touch them lightly, and finally complete their work with gentleness." Gerson (died 1429), chancellor of the University of Paris, in a work entitled "Bringing Children to Christ," recommended a mild discipline: "Above all, let the teacher try to be a father to his pupils. Let him never be angry with them. Let him always be simple in his instruction, and relate to his pupils that which is wholesome and agreeable."

In considering the favorable side of education during the Middle Ages, the Brethren of the Common Life, founded in the fourteenth century by Gerhard Groot, deserve especial mention. Without monastic vows, the members of this brotherhood led a life of purity, and labored with unselfish devotion for the good of others. They occupied themselves especially with the education of the poorer classes. Though the founder laid undue stress upon religious education, rejecting arithmetic, grammar, rhetoric, poetry, and geometry, the brotherhood afterwards departed from this narrowness, and included in their instruction a comprehensive course. Johannes Janssen, an able but partisan Roman Catholic writer, says: "In the schools of the brotherhood, Christian education was placed high above the mere acquisition of knowledge, and the practical religious culture of the youth, the nurture and confirmation of active piety, was considered the chief object. All the instruction was penetrated with a Christian spirit, and the pupil learned to regard religion as the most important human interest, and the foundation of all true culture. At the same time, a considerable amount of knowledge and a good method of study were imparted, and the pupil acquired an earnest love for literary and scientific activity. From all quarters, studious youth poured into their schools." *

A notable and lamentable fact in the educational arrangements of the Middle Ages was the neglect of the common people. No general effort was made to

---

* Janssen, Das deutsche Volk

reach and elevate them by education. The ecclesiastical schools were designed chiefly for candidates for the priesthood; the parochial schools fitted the young for Church membership; the burgher schools were intended for the commercial and artisan classes of the cities; knightly education gave a training for chivalry. Thus the laboring classes were left to toil on in ignorance and want; they remained in a dependent and servile condition, their lives unillumined by intellectual pleasures. If here and there, as claimed by Roman Catholic writers, popular schools were established, they were too few in number and too weak in influence to deserve more than passing mention. Popular education was the outgrowth of the Reformation.

At the beginning of the sixteenth century, the schools suffered from the corrupt condition of the Church. The ignorance of the clergy was reflected in the lives of their members. After visiting the churches and schools of Thuringia by order of the Elector John, Melancthon wrote: "What can be offered in justification, that these poor people have hitherto been left in such great ignorance and stupidity? My heart bleeds when I regard this misery. Often when we have completed the visitation of a place, I go to one side and pour forth my distress in tears. And who would not mourn to see the faculties of man so utterly neglected, and that his soul, which is able to learn and grasp so much, does not even know anything of its Creator and Lord?"

After the visitation of the churches of Saxony, in 1528, Luther wrote in the preface to his "Small Catechism:" "The pitiable need that I recently witnessed, as visitor, has compelled me to prepare this catechism on Christian doctrine in such simple form. Alas! what a sad state of things I witnessed! The common people, especially in the villages, are utterly ignorant of the Christian doctrine; even many pastors are wholly unqualified to teach; and yet all are called Christians, are baptized, and partake of the sacrament, knowing neither the Lord's Prayer, the Creed, nor the Ten Commandments, and living and acting like irrational brutes. Nevertheless, now that the precious Gospel has appeared again, they readily learn to abuse all freedom. O you bishops! how will you ever answer to Christ for having so shamefully neglected the people, and for not having exercised one moment your office that you might escape all evil?"

The following passage from Luther, in which he speaks of the improvements made in the universities by the Humanists and Reformers, throws light upon the higher education during the preceding period: "Almighty God has truly granted us Germans a gracious visitation, and favored us with a golden opportunity. We now have excellent and learned young men, adorned with every science and art, who, if they were employed, could be of great service as teachers. Is it not well known that a boy can now be so instructed in three years, that at the age of fifteeen or eighteen he knows more than all the universities and convents have known heretofore? Yea, what have men learned hitherto in the universities and monasteries, except to be asses and blockheads? Twenty, forty years it has been necessary to study, and yet one has learned neither Latin nor German. I say nothing of the shameful and vicious life in those institutions by which our worthy youth have been so lamentably corrupted."*

---

* Letter to the Mayors and Aldermen in behalf of Christian Schools.

CHAPTER V.

LUTHER.

IT is interesting to study the heroes of an epoch. While acted on by their surroundings—the state of society, the grade of culture, the views of the age—they become themselves the sources of a new creative power. Such heroes are at once an effect and a cause. Closely considered, they are found to exhibit, on the one hand, an immense receptivity, and, on the other, a large executive energy. They gather into themselves the thought and feeling of their age. They become the organs through which the spirit of the time finds utterance. They organize the movements that give satisfaction to the longings of the people. Speaking from the fulness of a rich inner experience, or from the certitude of intuitive knowledge, they acquire the authority of seers. They may not at first understand the full significance of their opinions and acts; but because they are loyal to the truth, they move forward in a straight line to the goal. Coming into conflict with existing institutions, they make enemies; laying broad and deep the foundations of human progress, their lives are filled with labor and care: but undaunted by foes and indifferent to toil, they follow their course with unconquerable determination. Their lives may end at the block or on the cross, but they remain loyal to their mission, the creators of eras, and the benefactors of mankind. These truths are illustrated in Martin Luther, the great hero of the sixteenth century. The story of his life is the history of the Reformation. Above all other men he embodied in himself the noblest tendencies of his time; and with marvelous penetration separating truth from error, he began and directed the movement that marks a new era in human progress.

Every nationality has its peculiar traits, which are inherited, to a greater or less degree, by each individual. It is to Luther's honor that he was the most German of Germans—one in whom the noblest characteristics of his race, in unity with Christian faith, found complete expression. No manlier type of character can be conceived. Fearless courage is united with tender sensibility. An indomitable spirit of independence co-exists with loyal submission to recognized authority. Strong passions are kept under by a deep piety. A passion for exciting amusements is regulated by a sturdy sense of duty. Convivial and social gayety is balanced by profound reflection and deep moral earnestness. Luther was the manliest of men, the ideal German, the great prophet of his people.

It has been said that God accomplishes his work by the weakest instrumentalities. In one sense this is true. The great providential men of our race have usually sprung from a lowly origin. Moses and David were shepherds; the apostles were fishermen; Christ was a carpenter; and Luther the son of a poor miner. But when these weak instrumentalities have once received the divinely appointed preparation for their work, they are no longer weak. They are changed into men of wide experience, keen insight, and steadfast character. The rude ore is transmuted into steel. The early career of the German Reformer was admirably adapted to fit him for his mission. He gradually rose from a lowly station to a position of commanding influence, and thus swept a wide range of human experience. The struggles of his early life imparted strength and solidity to his character. He was brought up in an atmosphere of deeply earnest but austere piety. His early school days at Mansfield were darkened by harsh discipline and crude methods of instruction. Destined to a learned career, he was sent, at the age of fourteen, to the school at Magdeburg conducted by the Brethren of the Common Life, and a year later he was removed to the school at Eisenach, presided over by John Trebonius, a learned Humanist and celebrated teacher. In both towns he had to beg for bread—a trial to which he pathetically referred in after life. "Do not despise the boys," he says, "who beg from door to door 'a little bread for the love of God' . . . I have myself been such a beggar pupil, and have eaten bread before houses, especially in the dear town of Eisenach."* Quick of comprehension and gifted in oratory, he excelled all his fellow-pupils. He completed his studies, which included logic, rhetoric, physics, and the ancient languages, at the University of Erfurt, and broadened his culture still further by extensive reading, especially in the scholastic philosophy. His ability attracted attention. Once very sick and in fear of death, he was comforted by an aged priest: "My dear bachelor, do not despair; you will not die of this illness; our God will yet make a great man of you, and you shall comfort many people. For our God permits those whom he loves and whom he wishes to use for great and good purposes to bear the holy cross; and those that in this school of trial patiently submit, learn much." It was in the library of the University that Luther one day discov-

---

*Sermon on the Duty of Sending Children to School.

ered a Bible, a copy of which, though in his twentieth year, he had never seen before.

Under the influence of deep religious convictions he entered the cloister at Erfurt, where he studied the Bible with such energy and success that he could at once refer to any passage in it. He passed through a profound religious experience, which issued at last in the doctrine of justification by faith. Called as professor to the newly founded University of Wittenberg, he lectured first on the dialectics and physics of Aristotle, and afterwards on the Scriptures. "This monk," the rector was accustomed to say, "will confound all our doctors, establish new doctrines, and reform the whole Roman church; for he bases himself on the writings of the prophets and apostles, and is firmly planted on the Word of Jesus Christ." A journey to Rome opened Luther's eyes to the corrupt state of the Papacy, and an official visitation of the Augustine monasteries in Meissen and Thuringia revealed to him the sad condition of the Church at large.

When in 1517 he began the great work of the Reformation by attacking Tetzel's sale of indulgences, he was not a novice, but a man of wide knowledge, clear convictions, and sturdy character. The fullness of time having come, he was ready, like another Moses, to deliver the people from bondage. Throughout his heroic struggle with the Papacy, he shows himself clear in vision, exhaustless in resources, and inflexible in purpose—the one Titanic form on the crowded canvas of the sixteenth century.

A petty intriguer can never be great. The habit of scheming gradually undermines the character, and at last destroys the power to cherish a magnanimous purpose, and the steadfast will to execute it. No other man ever had less of the intriguing spirit than Luther. The great foundation of his character was honesty. The first necessity with him was truth, and in its power and ultimate triumph he had unwavering confidence. Through trying spiritual conflicts he had been brought to an understanding of the Gospel. Its truth was certified in the depths of his soul. Though it was in fundamental conflict with the existing ecclesiastical system, he proclaimed it with uncompromising firmness. There was no indecision or duplicity in his character. Despising underhand methods, he did not seek to attain his ends by cajoling friends and flattering princes. He stood in striking contrast with Erasmus. The latter said: "As for me, I have no inclination to risk my life for the truth. We have not all strength for martyrdom; and if trouble come, I shall imitate Peter. Popes and emperors must settle creeds. If they settle them well, so much the better; if ill, I shall keep on the safe side." With a genuine martyr spirit, Luther forgot self in his devotion to truth; it was more to him than comfort, high position, or the favor of rulers; and in defiance of threatened dungeon and stake, he held to his testimony. His conscience was a strong factor in his mental life; and indifference to truth or selfish prudence in the presence of duty was regarded as a wrong to the Church, a blow at society, and an offense to God.

Nothing great can be accomplished without faith. It enters largely into the character of every hero— faith in one's cause, in one's strength, in one's destiny. No other faith imparts such adamantine firmness to character as faith in God. Let a man profoundly believe that the Almighty is his refuge and strength, and he becomes invincible. Luther was a man of preeminent faith. To him the presence and protection of God were realities. His faith shines forth in his writings and in his actions. His battle hymn of the Reformation expresses, not a poetic fancy, but a profound conviction:

> " A mighty fortress is our God,
> A bulwark never failing;
> Our helper he amid the flood
> Of mortal ills prevailing.
> * * * *

> And though this world, with devils filled,
>   Shall threaten to undo us,
> We will not fear, for God hath willed
>   His truth to triumph through us."

In the greatest trials and dangers, this faith gave him unfailing strength and joy. At an early stage of the Reformation, a papal legate came to Germany to silence the troublesome monk. Remonstrances, threats, entreaties, and even bribes were tried, but all in vain. Unless convinced of error, the Reformer remained immovable. He resisted the entreaties and defied the power of the sovereign of Christendom. At length the legate lost his temper, and exclaimed: "What do you think the Pope cares for the opinion of a German boor? The Pope's little finger is stronger than all Germany. Do you expect your princes to take up arms to defend you—a wretched worm like you? I tell you no! And where will you be then—where will you be then?" Sustained by his sublime faith, Luther calmly replied: "Then, as now, in the hands of Almighty God."

The two characteristics just considered—honesty and faith—naturally produce courage. If a man's conscience is clear and he gives his life to God, he can not be otherwise than courageous. He may not court danger, but when it comes in the line of duty, he will not run away. Luther was among the bravest of men. The gigantic undertaking to reform the Church exhibits in itself heroic courage. A miner's son, a simple priest, a young professor, assumes to instruct Christendom and overthrow the power of the Pope! A timid man like Melanchthon and a prudent man like Erasmus would have been appalled at the idea. Luther bravely pursues his purpose—teaches the truth in the lecture-room, thunders it from the pulpit, scatters it abroad by the press. When the storm comes he does not hide. Summoned to the imperial Diet at Worms, he was warned that he would be foully dealt with. Feeling it his duty to go, he replied: "Though they should kindle a fire that should rise up to heaven between Wittenberg and Worms, yet, as I am cited, I would appear there and step into the mouth of behemoth, confess Christ, and leave the issue to him." How grandly he bore himself before the Diet! The world has seen no sublimer spectacle since Paul made Felix tremble, or the King of the Jews stood before the Roman governor.

But Luther was not perfect—a fact that brings him nearer to ourselves. We can sympathize with Lessing, himself a great German, who after narrating an instance of the Reformer's intolerance, said: "I hold Luther in such reverence that I like to discover some faults in him. The traces of humanity that I find in him are to me as precious as the most dazzling perfections." Luther's character was not free from violence. His zeal for the truth, for the welfare of the Church, and for the prosperity of Germany, sometimes rendered him terrific; and in his wrath, he scourged his opponents—the Pope, Henry VIII., and the "robber peasants"—with a scorpion lash. Nothing can surpass the fury with which he attacked the peasant insurgents: "I think there are no more devils in hell, but all have gone into the peasants. . . . Whoever is slain on the side of the magistrates is a veritable martyr of God, if he fights with a good conscience. Whoever perishes on the side of the peasants will burn everlastingly in hell, for he is a limb of the devil. . . . Such times have come that a prince can serve heaven better with bloodshed than others with prayer. . . . Therefore, dear lords, let him who can thrust, strike, and kill. If meanwhile you are slain, more blissful death you could not undergo."* After the issue of the Reformation had been fully joined, Luther came to look upon the Papacy as Anti-Christ. His anger is excited at the mention of the name, and he freely uses harsh and opprobrious terms. His strong feeling sometimes leads him to exaggerated statements. Yet his vio-

---

*Schrift wider die räuberishen Bauern.

lence came less from native asperity than from ardent zeal. It may generally be regarded as the righteous indignation of a mighty soul deeply moved. His furious writing against the peasants originated in a deep concern for the imperilled social order. He was conscious of his harshness and violence; and in the following passage he not only admirably characterizes his style, but skillfully suggests an apology: "I seek not to flatter or to deceive you, and I do not deceive myself when I say that I prefer your writings to my own. It is not Brentius whom I praise, but the Holy Ghost who is gentler and easier in you. Your words flow pure and limpid. My style, rude and unskillful, vomits forth a deluge, a chaos of words, boisterous and impetuous as a wrestler contending with a thousand successive monsters; and if I may presume to compare small things with great, methinks there has been vouchsafed me a portion of the four-fold spirit of Elijah, rapid as the wind and devouring as fire, which roots up mountains and dashes rocks to pieces; and to you, on the contrary, the mild murmur of the light and refreshing breeze. I feel, however, comfort from the consideration that one common Father hath need, in his immense family, of each servant; of the hard against the hard, the rough against the rough, to be used as a sharp wedge against hard knots. To clear the air and fertililize the soil, the rain that falls and sinks like the dew is not enough—the thunderstorm is still required."*

There is no other intellectual quality so valuable as what is called common sense. In its highest form, it involves great mental vigor, as exhibited in keen penetration, retentive memory, strong feeling, and powerful will. It requires not only native symmetry of the faculties, but also regularity in their operation. Genius generally implies something abnormal—the development of a single faculty at the expense of others. On its strong side it is independent and brilliant, but often unsteady and eccentric. It is capable of high results in a single direction, but unfit to control a multitude of interests. Luther was not a genius; but no one since St. Paul has excelled him in massive intellectual strengh and soundness of judgment. He was distinguished as a student. In the writings of his mature years there is astounding vigor. The Reformation brought him innumerable perplexities; scholars, princes, and cities were constantly seeking his advice; the direction of the whole movement in Germany was largely in his hands: yet he seldom made a mistake. His mind was not metaphysical, but practical; he had no taste for fine-spun and

---

*Vorrede über Joh. Brentii Auslegung des Propheten Amos.

fruitless theories. At the university, like Lord Bacon a century later, he acquired a strong dislike for Aristotle and the schoolmen. He could not endure their fallacious subtleties. He was made, not for speculation, but for action; he constantly deals with the concrete—not with theories, but with conditions and facts. His style abounds in particular rather than in general terms. He possessed in an extraordinary degree the power to get at the heart of a matter—to lay firm hold upon the essential truth, and to lop off error. His intellectual range was of the broadest. He treated upon a vast number of subjects, yet with such skill and judgment that his works are still a rich store-house of wisdom. An acquaintance with the large folios that embody the achievements of his massive intellect, forces the conviction that Luther was the greatest of all Germans.

It adds to our conception of Luther's greatness that all his mental life was not absorbed in oaken sturdiness. He was sensitive to æsthetic pleasures. His character is like a Swiss landscape, where blooming valleys and plashing streams soften the rugged grandeur of snow-capped heights. He had a close sympathy with nature. At Coburg, where he stayed during the weighty proceedings of the Diet at Augsburg, he observed and playfully described a congress of jays and crows. When his old servant Lieberger was preparing some bird-snares, the Reformer drew up and presented to him, in behalf of the thrushes, blackbirds, finches and jays, a formal protest against his cruelty. While confined at the Wartburg, he once went out hunting with some friends, but his sympathy was with the game. "Notwithstanding the pleasure the spectacle afforded me," he says, "the spiritual application gave me equal pain. For it represents the devil, who, with insidious art, through his ungodly servants, hunts innocent souls to death. . . . At my instance we had preserved alive a little hare, and having enveloped it in the sleeve of my coat, I had gone away and left it for a short time; meanwhile the hounds traced up the poor animal, bit it through the coat, and killed it. Thus do the Pope and Satan rave, so that they destroy rescued souls and render all my labors vain." Watching the swelling buds one April day, Luther exclaimed: "Praise be to God the Creator, who out of a dead world makes all alive again. See those shoots how they bourgeon and swell! Image of the resurrection of the dead! Winter is death—summer is the resurrection. Between them lie spring and autumn as the period of uncertainty and change." In the following passage, what a fine appreciation of beauty! "If a man could make a single rose, we should give him an empire; yet roses, and other flowers no less beautiful, are scattered in profusion over the world, and no one regards them!" Luther was fond of music; he was a good singer and skillful player on the flute. Alone or in the company of friends he often sought recreation from his severe labors in the pleasures of vocal and instrumental music. He set a high value on its elevating influence. "Music," he said, "is one of the noblest and most delightful gifts of God; Satan is a great enemy to it; it is a good antidote against temptation and evil thoughts; the devil does not stay where it is practiced."

It is a question whether or not Luther was a poet. A recent writer has said that the Reformer "was neither a philosopher nor poet."* The truth of this statement depends upon our conception of the poetic gift. If we hold with Macaulay that "no person can be a poet . . . without a certain unsoundness of mind," we must refuse that distinction to Luther. No one was ever sounder. Neither does he correspond to Shakespeare's beautiful description of the poetic character:

>"As imagination bodies forth
>The forms of things unknown, the poet's pen
>Turns them to shapes, and gives to airy nothing
>A local habitation and a name."

---

*Hosmer, History of German Literature.

Luther did not possess the "fine frenzy" that reaches the highest lyrical achievement. His muse employed not a soft Æolian harp with its delicate and scarcely audible harmonies, but a great trumpet that called the nations to battle. He possessed an epic character— himself fitted to be an epic hero. He deliberately set himself to the task of supplying the German people with "spiritual songs, whereby," as he said, "the Word of God might be kept alive among the people by singing." For this task no one was better qualified. He had a profound experimental knowledge of the truth, an unrivalled mastery of the German tongue, and an unerring artistic sense. In all he composed or remodeled only thirty-seven hymns; but they were fashioned with such skill that they at once took hold of the popular heart. They were sung in the congregation, in the school, in the family, and became a powerful instrumentality for promoting the doctrines of the Gospel. Coleridge says that "Luther did as much for the Reformation by his hymns as by his translation of the Bible," and a Jesuit declares that "The hymns of Luther have killed more souls than his books and speeches." Energy of thought and feeling characterizes his hymns. No morbid sensibility in the presence of real or fancied ills, but a heroic faith and courage bent upon battle and victory. Thor

5*

himself could not have written with more overpowering energy.

The domestic life of Luther is very pleasing. The home he established with his Katie, as he called her, was almost ideal. He spoke from his experience in saying that "When marriage is peaceful and agreeable, it is, next to a knowledge of God and his Word, the highest favor and blessing." While his wife was affectionate, sensible, and thrifty, he was tender, appreciative, and magnanimous. Their household was well-ordered, cheerful, and hospitable. While exercising a salutary discipline, he was fond of children, and entered heartily into their sports. "The faith and life of children," he said, "are the best, for they have nothing but the Word. To this they cleave with simplicity, giving God the honor that he is true, being assured that he will do what he promises. But we old fools are subject to wretched, infernal doubt, which causes us first to dispute long about the Word, which the children receive simply in pure faith without disputing." His letter to his little son, written at Coburg, shows his deep sympathy with child nature. He was fond of companionship, and often had his friends with him at table. The meals were enlivened with music, humor, and profitable conversation. On such occasions Luther's ability appeared to great advantage, and his table-talk became famous for its freshness, originality, and depth. How tenderly human the great Reformer appears at the death-bed of his little daughter Magdalena. The strong man bowed his head. "I love her very dearly," he said, "but, dear God, since it is thy will to take her hence, I am glad to know that she will be with thee." Then turning to the bed, "Dear Magdalena, my daughter, you would like to remain here with your father, but you also go willingly to yonder Father?" "Yes, dearest father," the little girl said, "as God wills it." Then the father said; "Thou dear child, the spirit is willing, but the flesh weak." Turning away he said, "Oh, she is so dear to me! If the flesh is so strong, what will not the spirit be?" As Magdalena was breathing her last, the father in tears fell on his knees, and prayed God to release her. Thus she died, going to sleep in her father's arms. When the child lay in her coffin, Luther said, "Lena darling, how well it is with thee! Thou wilt rise again, and shine as a star—yes, as the sun—but the parting vexes me beyond measure. It is strange to know that she is certainly at peace, and that it is well with her, and yet be so sad!"

The highest eloquence is not a trick of language; it can not be attained merely by a skillful marshaling of words. True eloquence has its basis in energy of thought and feeling. Luther was gifted, perhaps, beyond any other man of his time as an effective speaker. His wide range of knowledge and experience rendered him exhaustless in ideas, while his intense fervor and depth of emotion sent forth his thoughts with tremendous force. His appearance was imposing, and his voice clear and sonorous. He was thoroughly natural; his diction was adapted to the thought; and when he spoke, he poured all the energy of his nature through a facile medium into the minds of his hearers. He was the greatest preacher of his age. The glowing tribute of Melanchthon seems hardly too strong: "One is an interpreter; another a logician; and still another an orator, affluent and beautiful in speech; but Luther is all in all—whatever he writes, whatever he utters, pierces to the soul, fixes itself like arrows in the heart—he is a miracle among men." In the proud independence of an intellectual and Christian freeman, he was unfettered by the traditions of the past, and judged all questions for himself. He cared little for the opinions of the Church fathers; having tested their teaching by the Word of God, he had often found them wrong. Yet he was in the noblest sense conservative. He was not an iconoclast and fanatic. His work was not destruction, but reformation; and even under the strongest provocation and excitement, he did not run into extravagance. His judgment always retained the ascendency; and though inflexible in his opposition to Romanism, he did not hesitate to chastise with extreme severity the dangerous aberrations of Protestant fanatics. In the presence of the Zwickau prophets, Melanchthon wavered; but Luther stood firm as a rock, unmasking and condemning their deluded or hypocritical pretensions. He could not be turned aside from the truth. He was the only man of the sixteenth century that had the wisdom and strength to lead the battle of the Reformation. Everywhere on the extended field his vigilant eye observed the complex movements of the opposing forces, and his brain directed and his voice cheered the great Protestant army of Germany. Alexander, Cæsar, and Napoleon are the world's ablest martial chieftains; yet their work was safety and simplicity itself compared with that of Luther—the thinker, the orator, the leader of the Reformation.

As in almost everything else, Luther was great in industry. His writings fill twenty-four folio volumes. With his life filled with practical duties, it is almost incomprehensible how he could accomplish so much with his pen. The secret lies in his indefatigable industry, that allowed no moment to escape unimproved. Here is his apology to his printer for some oversights in his manuscript: "I am very busily employed—I preach twice every day, I labor at the Psalter, I am engaged on postils, I reply to my adversaries, I contend against the bull of excommunication in German and Latin, and defend myself, not to mention the letters which I have to write to my friends, and the conversations that occur at home and elsewhere." This was written at an early stage of his career; and as in every busy and useful life, labors and cares increased with his years. He toiled with almost superhuman effort in his translation of the Bible. "Alas!" he said, "what a great and difficult task it is to make these Hebrew writers speak German—how reluctant they are to forsake their Hebrew ways and suit themselves to our rude German, just as if you would compel the nightingale to cease from her melodious strains, and to imitate the monotonous and odious cry of the cuckoo." Again he said: "I diligently exercised myself to employ pure and distinct German; and it often happened to us that we were two, three, and four weeks searching and inquiring for a single word, and after all sometimes failed to find it. In Job, Melanchthon, Aurogallus and myself encountered so many difficulties that we sometimes scarcely finished three lines in four days." After such conscientious and laborious effort, no wonder that his translation is a marvel of fidelity and excellence. But we are not to look for this painstaking care in his own productions. He wrote from an overflowing fulness of mind and heart; he was not forced to seek for ideas, but rather found difficulty in mastering the copious fountain that welled up in his soul. He spoke from an inner necessity. His pen dashed furiously across the page; he did not stop to refine and polish his language as did Melanchthon, but let his thoughts clothe themselves as best they could. His style is sometimes diffuse; it is not always clear; the construction is occasionally confused; and yet his writings never fail of their mark. A resistless energy of soul vibrates in every paragraph; it bears down opposition, and forces conviction. The style is the man. It bends with every changing emotion; sometimes, when the great soul of the writer is shaken with a mighty thought or emotion, it thunders and crashes like the storm; and again, when a buoyant joy has settled down upon his heart, it gently plashes like the wavelets of a sun-lit sea.

Such was Martin Luther. The ablest writers of modern times—historians, philosophers, theologians, poets—have eulogized his character and work. His life kindles admiration. No epic hero was ever greater. A man among men, yet towering above them in unapproachable grandeur. Holding the destiny of nations in his hand, he was calm and steadfast in God. Conscious at last of his divine mission, he esteemed his life as nothing. What power of thought and range of knowledge! He was inspired with the inspiration that comes from deep communion with God. His heart measured up to the full size of his capacious intellect. After wrestling with the mightiest sovereign of Christendom, and humbling his pride, he went home to play with his children. Matchless courage and strength united with childlike simplicity and tenderness! His life was unselfish consecration to truth. Look at him as we will, he stands out in solitary grandeur. In the language of Carlyle, whose study of the Reformer is admirably sympathetic and just: "I will call this Luther a true great man; great in intellect, in courage, affection, and integrity, one of our most lovable and precious men. Great, not as a hewn obelisk, but as an Alpine mountain—so simple, honest, spontaneous, not setting up to be great at all; there for quite another purpose than being great! Ah yes, unsubduable granite, piercing far and wide into the heavens; yet in the clefts of it fountains, green and beautiful valleys with flowers! A right spiritual hero and prophet; once more, a true son of nature and fact, for whom these centuries, and many that are to come yet, will be thankful to heaven."*

---

*Carlyle, Heroes and Hero-Worship. Lecture IV.

CHAPTER VI.

LUTHER ON DOMESTIC TRAINING.

LUTHER was gifted with great soundness of judgment, and was penetrated by the letter and spirit of Scripture. These two facts determine the character of his writings, and give them permanent value. In the existence of the sexes he saw the natural basis of marriage, and in revelation he found it a divine institution. The vices of the monks and Romish clergy exhibited the demoralizing effects of the unnatural law of celibacy. Hence, both by his example and in his writings, Luther defends what nature and God alike enjoin. In this he shows himself in advance of the Roman Catholic Church, which, while making marriage a sacrament, pronounces celibacy better. To select but a single passage from many, Luther says, "Next to God's Word, the world has not a more lovely and endearing treasure on earth than the holy state of matrimony, which He has Himself instituted, preserving it, having adorned and blessed it above all stations, from which not only all emperors, kings, and saints, but even the eternal Son of God, though in a supernatural way, are born. Whoever, therefore, hates the married state, and speaks evil of it, certainly is of the devil."

Luther had a clear conception of the constitution of society. He recognized the existence of the family, the State, and the Church, which he calls "three hierarchies established of God;" and the functions pertaining to these separate spheres, taken together, constitute the sum of human duty. The basis of both the State and the Church is found in the family, in which the young are to be trained for civil life and the Kingdom of God. "From the Fourth Commandment," Luther says, "it is obvious that God attaches great importance to obedience to parents. And where it is not found, there can be neither good morals nor good government. For where obedience is lacking in the family, no city or principality or kingdom can be well governed. Family government is the basis of all other government; and where the root is bad, the trunk and fruit can not be good.

"For what is a city but a collection of houses? How then can a city be well governed, when there is no government in the separate houses, and neither child nor servant is obedient? Likewise, what is a province but a collection of cities, towns, and villages? When, therefore, the families are badly controlled, how can the province be well governed? Verily there can be nothing but tyranny, witchcraft, murders, thefts, disobedience. A principality is made up of districts; a kingdom, of principalities; an empire, of kingdoms; these are all composed of families. Where the father and mother rule badly, and let the children have their own way, there neither city, town, village, district, principality, kingdom, nor empire, can be well and peacefully governed."

Luther set great store by the parental relation. "Oh, what a great, rich, and noble blessing," he exclaims, "God confers upon the married state! What joy does not a man experience in his descendants, who are numbered from him, even after his death." Again: "Children are the most lovely fruits and bonds of marriage, and confirm and preserve the bond of love." In his "Large Catechism," Luther begins his exposition of the Fourth Commandment with these words: "The parental estate God has especially honored above all estates that are beneath Him, so that He not only commands us to love our parents, but also *to honor* them. With respect to brothers, sisters, and our neighbors in general, He commands nothing higher than that we love them; so that He separates and distinguishes father and mother above all other persons upon earth, and places them next to himself. For *to honor* is far higher than *to love*, inasmuch as it comprehends not only love, but also modesty, humility, and deference as though to a majesty there hidden, and requires not only that they be addressed kindly and with reverence, but most of all that both in heart and with the body we so act as to show that we esteem them very highly, and that, next to God, we regard them the very highest."

The right training of children Luther enforces especially as a divine requirement. Parents are not free to do with their children as they please. They are entrusted with parental authority that they may train up their offspring for society and the Church, and they are held to a strict account for the manner in which they discharge this duty. This thought is presented again and again in Luther's writings. "But this is again a sad evil," he says, "that all live on as though God gave us children for our pleasure or amusement, and servants that we should employ them like a cow or ass, only for work, or as though all we had to do with our subjects were only to gratify our wantonness, without any concern on our part as to what they learn or how they live; and no one is willing to see that this is the command of the Supreme Majesty, who will most strictly call us to an account and punish us for it, nor that there is so great need to be so intensely anxious about the young. For if we wish to have proper and excellent persons both for civil and ecclesiastical government, we must spare no diligence, time, or cost in teaching and educating our children, that they may serve God and the world, and we must not think only how we may amass money and possessions for them. . . . Let every one know, therefore, that above all things it is his duty, (or otherwise he will lose the divine favor,) to bring up his children in the fear and knowledge of God; and if they have talents, to have them instructed and trained in a liberal education, that men may be able to have their aid in government and in whatever is necessary."

In this connection Luther's conception of religion appears in strong contrast with the works of human devising encouraged in the Romish Church. A right performance of domestic duties, particularly in the proper rearing of children, is better than fasting and pilgrimages. "Married people," Luther says, "should know that they can perform no better and no more useful work for God, Christianity, the world, themselves, and their children, than by bringing up their children well. Pilgrimages to Rome and to Jerusalem, building churches, providing for masses, or whatever else the work may be called, is nothing in comparison with the right training of children, for that is the straight road to heaven; and it can not be more easily attained in any other way. It is the peculiar work of parents, and when they do not attend to it, there is a perversion of nature, as when fire does not burn or water moisten. On the other hand, hell can not be more easily deserved, and no more hurtful work can be done, than by neglecting children, letting them swear, learn shameful words and songs, and do as they please."

Luther is not content with merely showing parents their duty, but with great earnestness he urges them to its performance. There is no argument that a comprehensive and thoughtful mind can adduce, that is not brought to bear upon them. The divine requirements are set forth; the evils resulting to society and the Church through neglect of their children are clearly pointed out; their gratitude to God and their obligations to mankind are urged as motives; and the guilt and punishment they bring upon themselves and their children are fully portrayed. As will be seen in the "Letter to the Mayors and Aldermen," and in the "Sermon on Sending Children to School," Luther in discussing this matter sometimes rises to an overmastering eloquence. A single passage from the "Large Catechism" will serve as illustration: "Think what deadly injury you are doing if you be negligent and fail to bring up your child to usefulness and piety, and how you bring upon yourself all sin and wrath, meriting hell even in your dealings with your own children, even though you be otherwise ever so pious and holy. And because this is disregarded, God so fearfully punishes the world that there is no discipline, government, or peace, of which we all complain, but do not see that it is our fault, for as we train them we have spoiled and disobedient children and subjects."

Luther recognizes the difficulties in the way of a salutary domestic training. Some parents are so lacking in piety that, like the ostrich, they harden themselves against their own offspring. Others by reason of their ignorance are unqualified to raise their children in a proper manner. And still others, who have the requisite piety and intelligence, are constantly burdened with cares and labors. Luther would have only such persons marry as are competent to instruct their children in the elements of religion. "No one should become a father," he says, "unless he is able to instruct his children in the Ten Commandments and in the Gospel, so that he may bring up true Christians. But many enter the state of holy matrimony who can not say the Lord's Prayer, and knowing nothing themselves, they are utterly incompetent to instruct their children. Children should be brought up in the fear of God. If the kingdom of God is to come in power, we must begin with children, and teach them from the cradle."

Luther naturally attached great importance to religious instruction. The truths of revelation—sin, redemption, judgment, eternal life—were to him supreme realities. Christianity is the power that regenerates our evil nature, fosters every virtue, and brings us into harmony with God. Whether we consider the present life or the life to come, it fits us for the highest usefulness and happiness. Religious instruction, therefore, becomes the first duty of the parental relation. "See to it," Luther says, "that you first of all have your children instructed in spiritual things, giving them first to God and afterwards to secular duties." "Children should be instructed in what pertains to God. They should be taught to know the Lord Jesus Christ, and constantly to remember how He has suffered for us, what He has done, and what He has promised. Thus were the children of Israel commanded to relate to their children and successors the miracles God had done for their fathers in Egypt. And when children have this knowledge, and yet do not learn to love and adore God, and to follow Jesus Christ, the punishment of God should be held up before them—His fearful judgment and anger at the wicked. If a person learns from youth up to recognize the benefits of God, and hence to love Him, and likewise the punishment and threatenings of God, and hence to fear Him, he will not forget it afterwards when he is old. For God will be honored in these two things, namely, that we love Him as a father for His blessings, and fear Him as a judge for His punishment."

The chief means of this religious instruction is the catechism, the principal parts of which are the Ten Commandments, the creed, and the Lord's Prayer. The head of the family should see to it that the children and servants thoroughly learn these leading articles of faith and duty. At least once a week he should examine them in order to ascertain what they have learned; and if they are not familiar with it, to keep them at it. Unwillingness to study the catechism Luther characterized as presumption, since it contains the fundamental articles of Christian belief and duty, and he himself set the example of reading and meditating upon it every morning. The Ten Commandments, the Creed, and the Lord's Prayer, says Luther, "are the most necessary parts, which every Christian should first learn to repeat word for word, and which our children should be accustomed to recite daily when they arise in the morning, when they sit down to their meals, and when they retire at night; and until they repeat them they should be given neither food nor drink. The same duty is also incumbent upon every head of a household, with respect to his man-servants and maid-servants, if they do not know these things and are unwilling to learn them. For a person who is so heathenish as to be unwilling to learn these things is not to be tolerated; for in these three parts everything contained in the Scriptures is comprehended in short, general, and simple terms."

Yet Luther would not have harshness employed in this religious instruction, knowing that rigorous severity is apt to defeat its purpose. On the contrary, he would have it made a pleasure to the children; and to this end we should adapt ourselves to their ways, prattle with them, and enter into their plays. Home should be made a delight; but at all times, in joy and in sorrow, the providence of God should be recognized. "We might thus," says Luther, "train our youth, in a childlike way and in the midst of their plays, in God's fear and honor, so that the First and Second Commandments might be familiar and in constant practice. Then some good might adhere, spring up and bear fruit, and men grow up in whom an entire land might rejoice and be glad. This would be the true way to bring up children; since, by means of kindness, and with delight, they can become accustomed to it. For what must only be forced with rods and blows will have no good result, and at farthest under such treatment, they will remain godly no longer than the rod descends upon their backs."

Luther's views of domestic discipline, based at once on nature and Scripture, were of the soundest. While strictly requiring obedience, parents should temper their government with moderation and love. We should curb and direct our children rather than break their spirit—a course that renders them pusillanimous. As Luther confesses, he suffered as a child from undue domestic rigor. In his own home at Wittenberg, while entering with delight into the pleasures of his children, he was strict in requiring obedience. He once refused for three days to receive an offending son into favor; and when Dr. Jonas and Dr. Teutleben interceded for the boy, Luther said, "I would rather have a dead than disobedient son." Commenting on Colossians iii. 21, "Fathers, provoke not your children to anger, lest they be discouraged," he says: "The injunction St. Paul here gives pertains to the mind; for of the body he in this place says nothing. He forbids that parents should provoke their children to anger, and thus discourage them. This is spoken against those who use passionate violence in bringing up their children. Such discipline begets in the child's mind, which is yet tender, a state of fear and imbecility, and develops a feeling of hate towards the parents, so that it often runs away from home. What hope can we have for a child that hates and distrusts its parents? Yet St. Paul does not mean that we should not punish children, but that we should punish them from love, seeking not to cool our anger, but to make them better."

The parent should understand his responsibility, and not ruin his child from a false tenderness. The soul of the child is more than the body, and its character should not be ruined through a neglect of the rod. Luther's nature was far too sound ever to sink into morbid sentimentality, and he quotes with approval the well known declaration of Solomon. "A false love," he says "blinds parents so that they regard the body of their child more than his soul. Hence the wise man says, 'He that spareth his rod hateth his son: but he that loveth him chasteneth him betimes' (Prov. xiii. 24) . . . . . Hence it is highly necessary that all parents regard the soul of their child more than his body, and look upon him as a precious, eternal treasure, which God has entrusted to them for preservation, so that the world, the flesh, and the devil do not destroy him. For at death and in the judgment they will have to render a strict account of their stewardship."

There are three ways in which parents ruin their children—by neglect, by bad example, and by worldly training. "Those parents that knowingly neglect their children and let them grow up without proper instruction, bring about their ruin; and though they do not set a bad example, yet they spoil their children by undue indulgence. . . . Such people as thus fondle and indulge their children must bear the sins of their children as if committed by themselves." "There are others who ruin their children by setting them a bad example in word and deed. . . . . There are people that are delighted when their sons are pugnacious and willing to fight, as if it were a great honor for them to be afraid of no one. Such people will in the end pay dearly for their folly, when they are called to mourn the untimely death that often with justice overtakes their sons. Young people are inclined to evil desires and to anger, and therefore it is necessary that parents should not excite them thereto by their example in word and deed. For when a child is accustomed to hear shameful words and oaths from its parents, what else can it learn but shameful words and oaths?" "The third class that ruin their children are those who teach them to love the world, and who have no other solicitude than that their children acquire an imposing bearing, learn to dance and dress, and cut a figure in society. We find but few at the present time who are as solicitous that their children be provided with those things that relate to God and the soul, as that they be provided with clothes, pleasures, wealth, and honor."

The sum of filial duty as enjoined in the Fourth Commandment is given by Luther as follows: "Learn, therefore, what is the honor toward parents required by this Commandment; first, that they be held in honor and esteemed above all things, as the most precious treasure on earth. Secondly, that in our words to them we observe modesty, and do not speak roughly, haughtily, and defiantly; but yield to them in silence, even though they go too far. Thirdly, also with respect to works, that we show them such honor with body and possessions, as to serve them, help them, and provide for them when old, sick, infirm, or poor, and all that not only gladly, but with humility and reverence, as doing it before God. For he who knows how to regard them in his heart will not allow them to suffer hunger or want, but will place them above and near him, and will share with them whatever he has and can obtain."

Interesting and valuable extracts might be indefinitely extended; but enough has been said to exhibit Luther's beautiful ideal of domestic life. Marriage is to be honored as a divine institution—the source of the highest earthly pleasures. The family occupies a fundamental relation to both civil and divine government, since it has the training of the future citizen and servant of God. By natural and divine right, authority is lodged in the parents, who occupy at once the threefold office of prophet, priest, and king. It is their function to instruct, to train, and to govern. The immediate end to be attained is the welfare and happiness of the family itself; and more remotely, the preparation of the young for useful and righteous living after their departure from the paternal roof. Children are to be regarded as a precious gift of God. Domestic government is to be administered in wisdom and love, which will prevent injustice, caprice, and passionate violence. The instruction of children, which should include every thing necessary for after life, should begin with religion as the most important of all subjects. The character should be based on a sense of personal obligation and responsibility to God, and the whole life be directed to a fulfilment of the divine commandments in all their relations. The parents should in all things set an example of upright living; and as long as the children are under parental control, they should be held to respect, love and obedience. Thus trained, they go forth into life to become honored and useful members of society.

CHAPTER VII.

LUTHER ON SCHOOLS.

Luther contributed in various ways to the advancement of education, and in this respect, as in many others, he rises high above all his contemporaries. With his usual penetration, he perceived at once the obligation and necessity of maintaining schools, and with powerful words urged this duty upon parents, cities, and princes. He pointed out the glaring defects of the schools of the time, and indicated improvements in both studies and methods. For religious instruction, which he made prominent, he wrote a catechism which, after the lapse of more than three centuries, has not been superseded in the large body of Protestants bearing his name. In co-operation with Melanchthon, he drew up plans for primary and secondary schools, and from the University of Wittenberg sent forth many enlightened and successful teachers. He pointed out with great clearness the fundamental truths, upon which all state and religious education must rest. If he did not emphasize education for its own sake, it was because his practical mind was obsorbed by the pressing needs of the time. Unfortunately, as often happens with great reformers, he was not fully understood by the men of his age; and this fact, in connection with the religious wars that followed after his death, prevented his ideas from being fully realized in practice. But even for the advanced pedagogy of to-day his writings contain many useful lessons.

Luther urged many considerations for the establishment of schools. On account of the religious disturbances, the educational institutions maintained under the Papacy were declining, and parents were becoming more indifferent. This neglect of education appeared to the Reformer as the work of the devil, who was thereby seeking the destruction of society and the Church. "Therefore I beg you all," says Luther, "in the name of God and of our neglected youth, not to think of this subject lightly, as do many who do not see what the prince of this world intends. For the right instruction of youth is a matter in which Christ and all the world are concerned. Thereby are we all aided. And consider that great Christian zeal is needed to overcome the silent, secret, and artful machinations of the devil. If we must annually expend large sums on muskets, roads, bridges, dams, and the like, in order that the city may have temporal peace and comfort, why should we not apply as much to our poor neglected youth, in order that they may have a skilful schoolmaster or two?"

The Germans ought to be moved, Luther said, to contribute of their means to the support of schools, because they had been relieved of papal exactions. The great opportunities afforded Germany by the Reformation should not be suffered to pass without improvement. "I believe Germany has never had so much of the Word of God," says Luther, "as at the present time; history reveals no similar period. If we let the gracious season pass without gratitude and improvement, it is to be feared that we shall suffer still more terrible darkness and distress. My dear countrymen, buy while the market is at your door; gather the harvest while the sun shines and the weather is fair; use the grace and Word of God while they are near. For know this, that the Word and grace of God are like a passing shower, which does not return where it has once been. The divine favor once rested upon the Jews, but it has departed. Paul brought the Gospel into Greece, but now they have the Turks. Rome and Italy once enjoyed its blessings, but now they have the Pope. And the German people should not think that they will always have it, for ingratitude and neglect will banish it." It is the will of God that children should be instructed, as is abundantly shown by Old Testament injunctions. In view of all these considerations, Luther's feelings were moved, and he exclaimed: "It is indeed a sin and shame that we must be aroused and incited to the duty of educating our children and of considering their highest interests, whereas nature itself should move us thereto, and the example of the heathen affords us varied instruction. There is no irrational animal that does not care for and instruct its young in what they should know, except the ostrich . . . And what would it avail if we possessed and performed all else, and became perfect saints, if we neglect that for which we chiefly live, namely, to care for the young? In my judgment there is no other outward offence that in the sight of God so heavily burdens the world, and deserves such heavy chastisement, as the neglect to educate children."

The two great reasons always prominent in Luther's mind for the maintenance of schools were the welfare of the Church and the needs of the State. Around these two central thoughts may be grouped nearly all that he wrote on education. His sermon on the "Duty of Sending Children to School"—his most extended educational treatise—is divided into (1) the spiritual, and (2) the temporal benefits of education. In the introduction to a treatise by Justus Menius,* Luther presents his views in a compendious manner: "This little book will be highly useful to heedless parents, that they may learn what God has commanded them concerning their children. If you have a child capable of learning, you are not free to bring it up as you please, or to deal with it according to your caprice, but you must consider that you are under obligation to God to promote both spiritual and secular government, and to serve Him thereby. God needs pastors, preachers, school teachers in His spiritual kingdom, and you can provide them; if you do not, behold, you rob, not a poor man of his coat, but the kingdom of God of many souls. . . . Thus, also, in secular government, you can serve your sovereign or country better by training children than by building castles and cities, and collecting treasures from the whole earth. For what good can these do, without learned, wise, and pious people?"

Schools help the Church by imparting a Christian training to children, by preparing useful teachers and heads of families, and by fitting ministers to preach and defend the Gospel. "When schools prosper," says Luther, "the Church remains righteous and her

---

*Vorrede zu Justi Menii Büchlein von Christlicher Haushaltung. 1529.

doctrine pure . . . . Young pupils and students are the seed and source of the Church. If we were dead, whence would come our successors, if not from the schools? For the sake of the Church we must have and maintain Christian schools. They may not appear attractive, but they are useful and necessary. Children are taught the Lord's Prayer and the Creed, and thus the Church is wonderfully aided through the primary schools."

Luther set a high value on the ministerial office, both because of its divine institution, and of its necessity for the advancement of the Church. He saw, too, in its religious teaching a strong support of civil order. Nothing can exceed the vigor with which he admonishes parents to give their sons to the ministry. They are reminded of their obligation to God, of the good they may accomplish through their children, and of the evil that will result from withholding them from the clerical office. "You have children and can give them," Luther says, "but will not do it; thus, so far as you are concerned, the ministry falls to the ground. And because you with gross ingratitude let the sacred office, so dearly purchased, languish and die, you will be accursed, and in your own person or in your children you will suffer shame and sorrow, or otherwise be so tormented that you will be damned with them not only here on earth but eternally in hell. This will not fail to come upon you, in order that you may learn that your children are not so entirely your own, that you can withhold them from God; he will have justice, and they are more His than yours."

It is a mistake to suppose, as some have done, that Luther was interested in education solely for the sake of the Church. His views were much too broad for that. He complained that the Papists conducted schools almost exclusively in the interests of the priesthood. He regarded civil government as a divine institution, and also as a necessary arrangement for social order and happiness. On both grounds it is to be maintained. Speaking of secular government, he says: "It is a beautiful and divine ordinance, an excellent gift of God, who ordained it, and who wishes to have it maintained as indispensable to human welfare; without it men could not live together in society, but would devour one another like irrational animals. Therefore as it is the function and honor of the ministerial office to make saints out of sinners, to restore the dead to life, and to confer blessedness upon the lost, to change the servants of the devil into children of God: so it is the function and honor of civil government to make men out of wild animals, and to restrain them from degenerating into brutes. It protects every one in body, so that he may not be injured; it protects every one in family, so that the members may not be wronged; it protects every one in house, lands, cattle, property, so that they may not be attacked, injured, or stolen."*

With such views of civil government, Luther was simply consistent when he said: "Even if there were no soul, and men did not need schools and the languages for the sake of Christianity and the Scriptures, still for the establishment of the best schools everywhere, both for boys and girls, this consideration is of itself sufficient, namely, that society, for the maintenance of civil order and the proper regulation of the household, needs accomplished and well-trained men and women. Now such men are to come from boys, and such women from girls; hence it is necessary that boys and girls be properly taught and brought up."†

Luther perceived the truth, which has become a maxim in modern education, that the welfare of a State depends on the intelligence and virtue of its citizens. As observation proved to him, this vital interest could not be wholly entrusted either to parents or the Church; the former would in many cases neglect it, and the latter too often pervert it. "Therefore it will

---

* Sermon on the Duty of Sending Children to School.

† Letter to Mayors and Aldermen in behalf of Christian Schools.

be the duty of the Mayors and Council," Luther says, "to exercise the greatest care over the young. For since the happiness, honor, and life of the city are committed to their hands, they would be held recreant before God and the world, if they did not, day and night, with all their power, seek its welfare and improvement. Now the welfare of a city does not consist alone in great treasures, firm walls, beautiful houses, and abundant munitions of war; indeed, where all these are found, and reckless fools come into power, the city sustains the greatest injury. But the highest welfare, safety, and power of a city consists in able, learned, wise, upright, cultivated citizens, who can secure, preserve, and utilize every treasure and advantage." It is to be noted, however, that in handing over education to the State, Luther did not contemplate, as will be readily understood, a complete secularization of the schools, but desired them to have a distinctly Christian character.

Education is an interest of such vital importance that it should be made compulsory. When towns and villages are able to maintain schools, the sovereign of the country has a right to compel them to do so, and likewise to require parents to send their children. In a letter to the Elector John in 1526, Luther says: "Where there are towns and villages which have the ability, your electoral grace has the power to compel them to maintain schools, pulpits, and parishes. If they will not do it from a consideration for their salvation, then your electoral grace, as highest guardian of the youth and of all others needing supervision, is to compel them to do so, just as they are compelled to render contributions and services toward bridges, paths and roads, or other matters pertaining to the public interest. Those that enjoy the privileges of a country, are to contribute towards everything that the common interests of the country require. Now there is nothing more necessary than to educate men who are to succeed us and govern." Again: "I maintain that the civil authorities are under obligation to compel the people to send their children to school, especially such as are promising, as has elsewhere been said. For our rulers are certainly bound to maintain the spiritual and secular offices and callings, so that there may always be preachers, jurists, pastors, scribes, physicians, schoolmasters, and the like; for these cannot be dispensed with. If the government can compel such citizens as are fit for military service to bear spear and rifle, to mount ramparts and perform other martial duties in time of war; how much more has it a right to compel the people to send their children to school, because in this case we are warring with the devil, whose object it is secretly to exhaust our cities and principalities of their strong men, to destroy the kernel and leave a shell of ignorant and helpless people, whom he can sport and juggle with at pleasure. That is starving out a city or country, destroying it without a struggle, and without its knowledge."*

An examination of Luther's pedagogical writings, shows that he had in mind three classes of schools, and thus a comprehensive system of education: 1. The Latin Schools, to which he gave most prominence; 2. The Universities, which he wished to see reformed; and 3. Schools for the common people, in which they might be fitted for the various callings of life. The fundamental principles of Protestantism, as we have already seen, logically issue in popular education—a fact that Luther clearly recognized. He repeatedly urged the establishment of schools for girls, which besides religious instruction were to include reading and writing. As early as 1520, in his Address to the Christian Nobility of the German Nation, he says: "Above all, in schools of all kinds the chief and most common lesson should be the Scriptures, and for young boys the Gospel; and would to God *each town had also a girls' school, in which girls might be taught*

---

*Sermon on Duty of Sending Children to School.

the Gospel for an hour daily, either in German or Latin! In truth, schools, monasteries, and convents were founded for this purpose, and with good Christian intentions, as we read concerning St. Agnes, and other saints; then were there holy virgins and martyrs, and in those times it was well with Christendom, but now it has been turned into nothing but praying and singing. Should not *every Christian* be expected by his ninth or tenth year to know all the holy Gospels, containing as they do his very name and life?" In a passage already quoted, Luther declares that the maintenance of civil order and the proper regulation of the household require "the establishment of the best schools everywhere, both for boys *and girls.*" In the constitution of the congregation at Leisnic, published and commended by Luther as a model, we find the following: "The ten directors, in the name of the congregation, shall have power to call, appoint, and remove a school teacher for the young boys. . . . In like manner the ten directors, out of the common treasury, shall provide an honorable, mature, and blameless woman to instruct young girls under twelve years of age in Christian discipline, honor, and virtue, and at a suitable place to teach them reading and writing in German a few hours daily." In a letter to the Elector John in 1530, Luther expressed his joy at the progress of education among the common people: "The tender youth of both sexes now grow up so well instructed in the catechism and Scripture, that my heart delights to behold how the boys and girls are able to pray, to exercise their faith, and to speak more of God and of Christ than all the cloisters, convents, and schools have hitherto been able to do."

Circumstances were allowed to determine the way in which schools should be supported. In some cases a tuition fee was charged, and in others the teacher was paid out of the common treasury of the congregation or State. The property of the cloisters, which in northern Germany had been emptied of monks and nuns, Luther desired to have appropriated to educational and ecclesiastical uses. This was done in many cases. The people were urged to contribute liberally to the support of schools, and Luther recommended education as a suitable object for bequests. "Therefore," says Luther, "let him who can, watch; and wherever the government sees a promising boy, let him be sent to school. If the father is poor, let the child be aided with the property of the Church. The rich should make bequests to such objects, as some have done, who have founded scholarships; that is giving money to the Church in a proper way. You do not thus release the souls of the dead from purgatorial fire, but you help, through the maintenance of divinely appointed offices, to prevent the living from going to purgatory; yea, you secure their deliverance from hell and entrance into heaven, and bestow upon them temporal peace and happiness. That would be a praiseworthy Christian bequest, in which God would take pleasure, and for which He would honor and bless you, that you might have joy and peace in Him."

Luther insisted on the importance of school training, as is shown in the following passage: "But each one, you say, may educate and discipline his own sons and daughters. To which I reply: we see indeed how it goes with this teaching and training! And when it is carried to the highest point, and is attended with success, it results in nothing more than that the learners, in some measure, acquire a forced external propriety of manner; in other respects they remain dunces, knowing nothing, and incapable of giving advice or aid. But were they instructed in schools or elsewhere by thoroughly qualified male or female teachers, who taught the languages, other arts, and history, then the pupils would hear the history and maxims of the world, and see how things went with each city, kingdom, prince, man and woman; and thus, in a short time, they would be able to comprehend as in a mirror, the character, life, counsels, undertakings, successes, and failures of the whole world from the beginning. From this knowledge they could regulate their views, and order their course of life in the fear of God, having become wise in judging what is to be sought and what avoided in this outward life, and capable of advising and directing others. But the training that is given at home is expected to make us wise through our own experience. Before that can take place, we shall die a hundred times, and all through life act injudiciously; for much time is needed to give experience."

Luther highly esteemed the office of teaching; he recognized not only its importance, but also its difficulties. "An industrious, pious school-master or teacher," he says, "who faithfully trains and educates boys, can never be sufficiently recompensed, and no money will pay him, as even the heathen Aristotle says. Yet the calling is shamefully despised among us, as if it were nothing, and at the same time we pretend to be Christians! If I had to give up preaching and my other duties, there is no office I would rather have than that of school-teacher. For I know that next to the ministry it is the most useful, greatest, and best; and I am not sure which of the two is to be preferred. For it is hard to make old dogs docile and old rogues pious, yet that is what the ministry works at, and must work at, in great part, in vain; but young trees, though some may break in the process, are more easily bent and trained. Therefore let it be considered one of the highest virtues on earth faithfully to train the children of others, which duty but very few parents attend to themselves."* And again: "I would have no one chosen for a preacher who has not previously been a school-teacher. But at the present time our young men want to become preachers at once, and to avoid the labor of school-keeping. When one has taught about ten years, then he can give it up with a good conscience; for the labor is too heavy and the appreciation is small. Yet a school-master is as important to a city as a pastor is. We can do without mayors, princes, and noblemen, but not without schools; for these must rule the world. We see to-day that there is no potentate or lord who is not ruled by a jurist or theologian; for they are ignorant themselves, and are ashamed to learn. Therefore schools are indispensable. And if I were not a preacher, there is no other calling on earth I would rather have. But we must consider, not how the world esteems and rewards it, but how God looks upon it."†

---

*Sermon on Duty of Sending Children to School.
†Aus den Tischreden.

The universities did not meet the requirements of Luther's practical mind. The principle of authority prevailed in them, to the suppression of independent investigation; the energy of the students was often wasted on useless or even frivolous questions; and the results attained in culture did not correspond to the outlay of time and effort. In his Address to the Nobility in 1520, Luther says: "The universities also require a good, sound reformation. This I must say, let it vex whom it may. The fact is that whatever the Papacy has ordered or instituted is only designed for the propagation of sin and error. What are the universities, as at present ordered, but as the Book of Maccabees says, 'schools of Greek fashion and heathenish manners,' full of dissolute living, where very little is taught of the Holy Scriptures and of the Christian faith, and the blind heathen teacher, Aristotle, rules even further than Christ. Now my advice would be that the books of Aristotle, the 'Physics,' the 'Metaphysics,' 'Of the Soul,' and 'Ethics,' which have hitherto been considered the best, be altogether abolished, with all others that profess to treat of nature, though nothing can be learned from them, either of natural or spiritual things. Besides, no one has been able to understand his meaning, and much time has been wasted, and many vexed with much useless labor, study, and expense."

As is evident from the foregoing survey, Luther approached education from the practical side. He was led to this aspect of the subject both by the native bent of his mind, and the urgent necessities of the Church and State. While recognizing education as a development or strengthening of our native powers, he directed his attention most to its character as a preparation for the various duties of life. He would have accepted Milton's definition as a clear embodiment of his views: "I call a complete and generous education that which fits a man to perform justly, skillfully and magnanimously all the offices, both private and public, of peace and war." He would have made no objection to the definition of Herbert Spencer—"Education is the preparation for complete living"— though differing from the Englishman in his conception of "complete living." He would have been pleased with Niemeyer's definition: "Education is at once the art and the science of guiding the young and of putting them in a condition, by the aid of instruction, through the power of emulation and good example, to attain the triple end assigned to man by his religious, social, and national destination." The schools of Germany to-day are but a realization, more or less complete, of Luther's ideas. He sought the establishment of primary schools for the instruction of the masses, that they might better discharge their domestic, religious, and social duties; he urged the necessity of secondary schools for those who were to pursue professional careers in Church and State; he defended the higher education of the universities, where the final preparation for learned vocations was to be obtained. In education, as in religion, Luther showed himself great, a seer in advance of his age, the founder of a new and higher culture.

CHAPTER VIII.

LUTHER ON STUDIES AND METHODS.

LUTHER had a profoundly religious nature, gave his life to religious interests, and saturated his thought and feeling with religious truth. He looked upon religion not only as the highest interest of life, but as the basis of all worthy living. It was natural, therefore, that he should emphasize religious instruction, and make the Scriptures prominent in schools of every grade. "Above all," he says, "in schools of all kinds the chief and most common lesson should be the Scriptures, and for young boys the Gospel; and would to God each town had also a girls' school, in which girls might be taught the Gospel for an hour daily, either in German or Latin! . . . But where the Holy Scriptures are not the rule, I advise no one to send his child. Everything must perish where God's Word is not studied unceasingly; and so we see what manner of men there are now in the universities, and all this is the fault of no one but the Pope, the bishops, and prelates, to whom the welfare of the young has been entrusted." "The soul can do without everything except the Word of God. Without this it suffers need. But when it has the Word of God, it needs nothing more, but has in the Word enough—food, joy, peace, light, art, righteousness, truth, freedom, and every good thing in abundance." To promote this knowledge of the Scriptures, to place this priceless treasure in the hands of the people, Luther translated the Bible, which was seized upon with such avidity that in a few years nearly half a million copies were in circulation. It became a mighty influence in Germany—an important factor in giving that country its present pre-eminence in Europe.

In teaching the Bible, Luther recognized the value of wide experience and extensive learning. "Whoever," he says, "is to teach others, especially out of the Holy Scriptures, and rightly to understand this book, must first have observed and learned to know the world." "One knife cuts better than another, and thus can one, who understands the languages and arts, speak and teach best." In preparation for teaching the Scripture, Luther recommends the most painstaking examination of the words of the text, as well as prolonged meditation in the heart. "You should not only consider the words in your heart, but examine them diligently as they stand in the text, that you may arrive at the meaning of the Holy Ghost. And see to it, that you do not become weary and imagine after reading it once or twice that you understand it thoroughly; for such a course makes, not profound theologians, but such as resemble unripe fruit that falls before its time."

Next to the Scriptures Luther attached importance to the Catechism, which he regarded as a brief summary of their teaching. Moved by the great ignorance he discovered during his visitation of the Saxony churches, he prepared in 1529 his two Catechisms, of which in three or four decades a hundred thousand copies were in use. In one of the prefaces, he says: "This little work has been planned and undertaken in order to furnish a course of instruction for children and the simple-minded. Hence, of old, such works received in Greek the name *Catechism, i. e.*, instruction, for children. This of necessity every Christian should know; so that he who does not know this should not be reckoned among Christians nor admitted to the Sacrament, just as a mechanic who does not understand the rules and customs of his trade, is rejected and regarded incapable. Therefore, the young should be thoroughly instructed in the parts which belong to the Catechism or instruction for children, and should diligently exercise themselves therein."

Very significant in relation to method are Luther's

directions for using the Catechism. His independent and practical mind is here clearly exhibited in discarding the harsh, mechanical, and uninteresting methods commonly in use in his day. In methods, as well as in studies, though sometimes falling into error, Luther deserves to be ranked with such educational reformers as Comenius and Pestalozzi. In the preface of his Small Catechism, he says: "In the first place, let the preacher take the utmost care to avoid all changes or variations in the text and wording of the Ten Commandments, the Lord's Prayer, the Creeds, the Sacraments, etc. Let him, on the contrary, take each of the forms respectively, adhere to it, and repeat it anew year after year. For young and inexperienced people can not be successfully instructed unless we adhere to the same text or the same forms of expression. They easily become confused when the teacher at one time employs a certain form of words and expressions, and at another, apparently with a view to make improvements, adopts a different form. The result of such a course will be that all the time and labor which we have expended will be lost." The pedagogical principle here involved may be stated thus: *In teaching children use simplicity and repetition.* It is correct. A hundred years later Ratich, who as an educational reformer occupies a respectable place in the History of Education, said: "Teach only one thing at a time, and often repeat the same thing." The wisdom of lodging truth in the young mind by means of a fixed form of words is often overlooked in the teaching of the present day.

Luther continues: "In the second place, when those whom you are instructing have become familiar with the words of the text, then teach them to understand the meaning of those words, so that they may become acquainted with the object and purport of the lesson... Allow ample time for the lessons. For it is not necessary that you should, on the same occasion, proceed from the beginning to the end of the several parts; it will be more profitable if you present them separately, in regular succession. When the people have, for instance, at length correctly understood the First Commandment, you may proceed to the Second, and so continue. By neglecting to observe this mode the people will be overburdened, and be prevented from understanding and retaining in memory any considerable part of the matter communicated to them." About the thoroughness here recommended there can be no question; but as a general rule, the deductive method, which begins with comprehensive statements, should not be used with children. The inductive method, as set forth by

Comenius in the following statement, is better adapted to child nature: "The concrete should precede the abstract; the simple, the complex; the nearer, the more remote." Yet, in a short Catechism like Luther's, it may be a question whether the deductive method is not, after all, the most economical and effective.

"In the third place," Luther says, "when you have reached the end of the Short Catechism, begin anew with the Large Catechism, and by means of it furnish the people with fuller and more comprehensive explanations." This gradation in study is wise. Luther did not contemplate a mere lifeless memorizing of the doctrines and explanations of the Catechism, but a practical and intelligent instruction that would bear fruit in every-day life. "Insist in an especial manner," he says, "on such commandments or other parts as seem to be most of all misunderstood or neglected by your people. It will, for example, be necessary that you should enforce with the utmost earnestness the Seventh Commandment, which treats of stealing, when you are teaching workmen, dealers, and even farmers and servants, inasmuch as many of these are guilty of various dishonest and thievish practices."

Luther understood the worth of the Socratic or question method as a means of awakening mind and impressing truth, and he recommends it in a writing*

---

* Von der deutschen Messe und Ordnung des Gottesdienstes.

published in 1526. After urging the necessity of home instruction for children and servants, he continues: "Not simply that they may learn and repeat the words by heart, as has hitherto been the case, but let them be questioned from article to article, and show what each signifies and how they understand it. If everything can not be asked at one time, take one article to-day, and another to-morrow. For when parents or guardians will not take the trouble through themselves or others, there no catechetical instruction can ever be successful." Then follows an illustration of how this instruction should be given. "The teacher should ask: 'What do you pray?' Answer: 'The Lord's Prayer.' 'What is meant by "Our Father who art in Heaven?"' Answer: 'That God is not an earthly, but a Heavenly Father, who will make us rich and blessed in Heaven.' 'What is meant by "Hallowed be Thy name?"' Answer: 'That we should honor His name that it may not be profaned.' 'How is it profaned?' Answer: 'When we, who are His children, lead evil lives, and teach and believe error.'" And so on with every statement in the Catechism.

Though living in a period of religious strife, it is to Luther's credit both as a Christian and teacher that he would not have the children perplexed with controversial questions. In the Saxony School Plan, it is said: "The school-master shall impress upon the children those truths that are necessary to right living, as the fear of God, faith, and good works. He shall not speak of polemical matters. He shall not, as many unskilful teachers do, accustom the children to hate the monks and others."

Luther was a careful observer of children, and wisely proposed to adapt his methods of instruction to their nature. In this he anticipated our modern pedagogy. In speaking of the severe punishment received in his childhood, he says of his parents that " they meant it perfectly well, but were not able, as regards *dispositions*, to observe the distinction, according to which punishment must be meted out." In the " Letter to the Mayors and Aldermen," he proposes to utilize the natural activity and acquisitiveness of children in education. "Now since the young must leap and jump, or have something to do, because they have a natural desire for it that should not be restrained, (for it is not well to check them in everything,) why should we not provide such schools, and lay before them such studies? By the gracious arrangement of God, children take delight in acquiring knowledge, whether languages, mathematics, or history." In the Large Catechism Luther lays down the important principle that learning should be made pleasant to children. "Since we are preaching to children, we must also prattle with them." " What must be forced with rods and blows will have no good result, and at farthest, under such treatment, they will remain godly no longer than the rod descends upon their backs." Elsewhere, after commending an interesting device (that of two little bags with pockets) for impressing the meaning of faith and love, Luther says: " Let no one think himself too wise, and disdain such child's play. When Christ wished to teach men, he became a man. If we are to teach children, we must become children. Would to God we had more of this child's play! We should then see in a short time a great treasure of Christian people, souls rich in the Scriptures and in the knowledge of God."

The value of concrete examples to illustrate and enforce abstract truth was clearly recognized by Luther. He recommends that in the explanation of his Catechisms many illustrations be drawn from the Scriptures. The utility of history consists partly in its serving to illustrate abstract statements and principles. "The celebrated Roman, Varro," Luther says in an interesting passage, "affirms that the best way to teach is to unite examples with words. This results in a clearer apprehension of what is taught, and secures also its better retention; otherwise, when statements are heard without examples, no matter how good the doctrine may be, the heart is not so deeply moved, and the subject is not so clearly understood nor so firmly retained. Therefore, history is very valuable. For whatever philosophy or reason teaches, that history supplies with illustrations, and portrays, as it were, before our eyes what the words convey to the ear. We there see how the good and the wise have lived, and how they have been rewarded; and also how the wicked and the ignorant have done, and how they have been punished."

Luther set great store by the ancient languages, not indeed for their superiority as an educational gymnastic, but for their utility in the service of the Church. In the "Letter to the Mayors and Aldermen," he discusses the matter fully. He esteems the ancient languages for their aid in understanding the Scriptures, and in carrying on the government. It was through them that the Gospel had been restored to the world in its purity, and through them it was to be preserved and extended. Elsewhere he says: "I do not hold with those who give themselves to one language, and despise all others. For I should like to bring up such people as can be of use to Christ in foreign lands, that it may not go with us as with the Waldenses in Bohemia, who confined their doctrine to their own language in such a way, that no one could clearly understand them without first learning their language. But the Holy Spirit acted differently; He did not wait till all the world came to Jerusalem and learned Hebrew, but He bestowed the gift of tongues upon the apostles, so that they could speak wherever they came. I prefer to follow this example, and hold it proper to exercise the young in many languages; for who knows how God may use them? For this purpose also schools are established." While emphasizing thus the importance of Latin, Greek, and Hebrew, in the interests of religion, Luther was also a great teacher of his native language. He introduced it into public worship, and encouraged the establishment of primary schools in which it was employed. Through his sermons, books, hymns, and especially his translation of the Bible, he gave the German language a literary form, and laid the basis of its cultivation and development. A few years after his death, John Clajus published a German grammar, in which the Reformer's language was taken as the standard.

In regard to the best methods of teaching languages, Luther laid down principles that are recognized as fundamental in modern educational science. In addition to the study of grammar, he calls attention to the value of practice, and distinguishes between a knowledge of words and a knowledge of things. The following extract is worthy of special attention: "Every one learns German or other languages much better from talking at home, at the market, or in the church, than from books. Printed words are dead, spoken words are living. On the printed page they are not so forcible as when uttered by the soul of man through the mouth. Tell me, where has there ever been a language that one could learn to speak properly from the grammar? Is it not true that even the languages that have the most clearly defined rules, as the Latin and the Greek, can be better learned from practice and habit than from rules? . . . The science of grammar teaches and shows what words are called and what they mean; but we should first of all learn the thing itself. Whoever is to preach and teach must know beforehand what a thing is and what it is called; but grammar teaches only the last. Knowledge is of two kinds—one of words, and the other of things. Whoever has no knowledge of the things will not be helped by a knowledge of the words. It is an old proverb that 'one can not speak well of what one does not understand.' Of this truth our age has furnished many examples. For many learned and eloquent men have uttered foolish and ridiculous things in speaking of what they did not understand. But whoever thoroughly understands a matter will speak wisely and reach the heart, though he may be wanting in eloquence and readiness of speech. Thus Cato surpassed Cicero when he spoke in council, though his language was simple and unadorned. A knowledge of words or grammar becomes easier when the subject in hand is understood, as Horace also teaches. But when a knowledge of the subject is wanting, then a knowledge of words is useless. I do not wish to be understood as rejecting grammar, which is necessary; but this I say: if the subject is not studied along with the grammar, one will never become a good teacher. For as some one has said, the teacher's or preacher's discourse should be born, not in his mouth, but in his heart."

Luther approved of rhetoric and dialectic, an old name for the practical part of logic. In both he was himself a master, as is abundantly evident from his writings. "Dialectic instructs," he says, "and rhetoric moves; the former appeals to the understanding, the latter to the will." But logic can not supply knowledge, it only shows us how to use it. "It does not give us the power to speak of all subjects, but is simply an instrument, by which we can speak correctly and methodically of what we already know and understand." Simple language is best. "One should accustom himself to good, honest, intelligible words, which are in common use and serve to elucidate the subject—a gift that comes from the grace of God. Many would-be scholars purposely obscure a subject with odd, unusual, and high-flown words, and seek a new style of discourse, which is yet so ambiguous and unintelligible that it can be understood as one pleases."

Luther looked upon history, not simply as a source of illustration for moral and philosophic truth—a benefit spoken of in a passage already quoted—but also as a portrayal of God's wonderful dealings with men and a leading source of human knowledge. He spoke in strong terms of its importance. When urging in his "Letter to the Mayors and Aldermen" the establishment of libraries, he said: "A prominent place should be given to chronicles and histories, in whatever languages they may be obtained; for they are wonderfully useful in understanding and regulating the course of the world, and in disclosing the marvelous works of God." Elsewhere he says more at length: "When one thoroughly considers the matter, it is from history, as from a living fountain, that have flowed all laws, sciences, counsel, warning, threatenings, comfort, strength, instruction, foresight, knowledge, wisdom, and all the virtues; that is to say, history is nothing else than an indication, recollection, and monument of divine works and judgments, showing how God maintains, governs, hinders, advances, punishes, and honors men, according as each one has deserved good or evil. And although there are many who do not recognize and regard God, yet must they take warning from history, and fear that it may go with them as with many a one therein portrayed, whereby they are moved more than by mere admonition in words; as we read not alone in the Holy Scriptures, but also in heathen books, how men introduced and held up the examples, words, and works of their ancestors, when they wished to accomplish something with the multitude, or to teach, admonish, warn, or terrify.

"Therefore historians are most useful people and most excellent teachers, whom we can never sufficiently honor, praise, and thank, and it should be a care of our great lords, as emperors and kings, to have histories of their times written and preserved in libraries, and they should spare no expense to procure persons capable of teaching. . . . But it requires a superior man to write history, a man with a lion-heart, who dares without fear to speak the truth. For most men write in such a way, that, according to the wishes of their rulers or friends, they pass over the vices or degeneracy of their times, or put the best construction upon them; on the other hand, through partiality for their fatherland and hostility to foreigners, they unduly magnify insignificant virtues, and eulogize or defame according to their preferences or prejudices. In this way histories become beyond measure untrustworthy, and God's work is obscured. Since history describes nothing else than the ways of God, that is, grace and anger, which we should believe as if they stood in Scripture, it ought to be written with extreme care, fidelity, and truth."*

Luther's attitude to the world of nature is full of interest, and exhibits both his independence of character and genuineness of feeling. He was brought up in schools in which, according to the methods of the Middle Ages, nature was studied, not by observing the earth, air, and skies, but by perusing the works of Aristotle and Pliny. It was the reign of words, not of things. Luther's great sympathetic heart could not be satisfied with this narrowness. His eyes were open to the beauty about him, and he beheld with tenderness the chattering birds, and the growing plants. His life was not abstraction, but observation. His style is concrete, full of images of things about him, and of words of the common people. He

---

*Vorrede D. M. L. auf die Historia Galeatii Capellæ vom Herzog zu Mailand. 1538.

recognized the intrinsic worth of the natural sciences, and in a passage exhibiting a truly prophetic spirit, he says: "We are at the dawn of a new era, for we are beginning to recover the knowledge of the external world that we had lost through the fall of Adam. We now observe creatures properly, and not as formerly under the Papacy. Erasmus is indifferent, and does not care to know how fruit is developed from the germ. But by the grace of God we already recognize in the most delicate flower the wonders of divine goodness and omnipotence. We see in His creatures the power of His word. He commanded, and the thing stood fast. See that force display itself in the stone of a peach. It is very hard, and the germ it encloses is very tender; but, when the moment has come, the stone must open to let out the young plant that God calls into life. Erasmus passes by all that, takes no account of it, and looks upon external objects as cows look upon a new gate." In this passage is foreshadowed the wide-reaching doctrine of Comenius—a doctrine very potent in moulding modern education: "Why shall we not, instead of dead books, open the living book of nature? Not the shadows of things, but the things themselves, which make an impression on the senses and imagination, are to be brought before youth. By actual observation, not by a verbal description of things, must instruction begin. From such observation develops a certain knowledge. Men must be led as far as possible to draw their wisdom not from books, but from a consideration of heaven and earth, oaks and beeches; that is, they must know and examine things themselves, and not simply be contented with the observation and testimony of others."*

Luther's love for music was remarkable. He had a good voice, and played skillfully on the guitar and flute. Among the loveliest scenes in his happy home at Wittenberg are those in which, in company with chosen friends, he sought recreation from his arduous labors in the holy joys of sacred song. The tributes he paid to music are many and beautiful. He desired the young to be diligently exercised in vocal and instrumental music, and insisted on musical attainments as an indispensable qualification in the teacher. His influence on the musical culture of Germany is important. By means of suitable hymns and tunes, many of which he composed himself, he popularized Church music and enabled worshiping congregations to unite in the singing. In the schools that were established under the influence of Luther and his co-adjutors, music formed a part of the regular course of

---

* Painter, History of Education, p. 209.

instruction. It was honored not only as a useful adjunct in public worship, but also as a source of beneficent influence upon the character and life. The following passages—a few out of many—will serve to show Luther's regard for music. "Satan is a great enemy to music. It is a good antidote against temptation and evil thoughts. The devil does not stay long where it is practiced." "Music is the best cordial to a person in sadness; it soothes, quickens, and refreshes his heart." "Music is a semi-disciplinarian and school-master; it makes men more gentle and tender-hearted, more modest and discreet." "I have always loved music. He that is skilled in this art is possessed of good qualities, and can be employed in anything. Music must of necessity be retained in the schools. A school-master must be able to sing, otherwise I will hear nothing of him." "Music is a delightful, noble gift of God, and nearly related to theology. I would not give what little skill I possess in music for something great. The young are to be continually exercised in this art; it makes good and skillful people of them." "With those that despise music, as all fanatics are wont to do, I am not pleased; for music is a gift bestowed by God and not by man. So it also banishes Satan, and renders men joyful; it causes men to forget all wrath, uncharity, pride, and other vices. Next to theology, I esteem and honor music. And we see how David and all the saints clothed their pious thoughts in verses, rhymes, and songs; because in times of peace music rules."

Luther encouraged gymnastic exercises, which he regarded salutary both for the body and the soul. "It was well considered and arranged by the ancients," he says, "that the people should practice gymnastics, in order that they might not fall into revelling, unchastity, gluttony, intemperance and gaming. Therefore these two exercises and pastimes please me best, namely, music and gymnastics, of which the first drives away all care and melancholy from the heart, and the latter produces elasticity of the body and preserves the health. But a great reason for their practice is that people may not fall into gluttony, licentiousness, and gambling, as is the case, alas! at courts and in cities. Thus it goes when such honorable and manly bodily exercises are neglected."

We leave it to the two treatises presented in the following chapters to supply what is lacking in this survey of Luther's pedagogy. Looking back over the ground traversed, we realize that the great Reformer accomplished scarcely less for education than for religion. Through his influence, which was fundamental, wide-reaching, and beneficent, there began for the one as for the other a new era of advancement. Let us note a few particulars:

1. In his writings, as in the principles of Protestantism, he laid the foundation of an educational system, which begins with the popular school and ends with the university.

2. He set up as the noble ideal of education *a Christian man*, fitted through instruction and discipline to discharge the duties of every relation of life.

3. He exhibited the necessity of schools both for the Church and the State, and emphasized the dignity and worth of the teacher's vocation.

4. With resistless energy he impressed upon parents, ministers, and civil officers their obligation to educate the young.

5. He brought about a re-organization of schools, introducing graded instruction, an improved course of study, and rational methods.

6. In his appreciation of nature and of child-life, he laid the foundation for educational science.

7. He made great improvements in method; he sought to adapt instruction to the capacity of children, to make learning pleasant, to awaken mind through skillful questioning, to study things as well as words, and to temper discipline with love.

8. With a wise understanding of the relation of

virtue and intelligence to the general good, he advocated compulsory education on the part of the State.

In view of these facts, Luther deserves henceforth to be recognized as the greatest, not only of religious, but of educational reformers.

CHAPTER IX.

LUTHER'S LETTER TO THE MAYORS AND ALDERMEN OF ALL THE CITIES OF GERMANY IN BEHALF OF CHRISTIAN SCHOOLS.

GRACE and peace from God our Father and the Lord Jesus Christ. Honored and dear Sirs: Having three years ago been put under the ban and outlawed, I should have kept silent, had I regarded the command of men more than that of God. Many persons in Germany both of high and low estate assail my discourses and writings on that account, and shed much blood over them. But God who has opened my mouth and bidden me speak, stands firmly by me, and without any counsel or effort of mine strengthens and extends my cause the more, the more they rage, and seems, as the second Psalm says, to "have them in derision." By this alone any one not blinded by prejudice may see that the work is of God; for it exhibits the divine method, according to which God's cause spreads most rapidly when men exert themselves most to oppose and suppress it.

Therefore, as Isaiah says, I will not hold my **peace**

until the righteousness of Christ go forth as brightness, and his salvation as a lamp that burneth.* And I beseech you all, in the name of God and of our neglected youth, kindly to receive my letter and admonition, and give it thoughtful consideration. For whatever I may be in myself, I can boast with a clear conscience before God that I am not seeking my own interest, (which would be best served by silence,) but the interest of all Germany, according to the mission, (doubt it who will,) with which God has honored me. And I wish to declare to you frankly and confidently that if you hear me, you hear not me but Christ; and whoever will not hear me, despises not me but Christ.† For I know the truth of what I declare and teach; and every one who rightly considers my doctrine will realize its truth for himself.

First of all we see how the schools are deteriorating throughout Germany. The universities are becoming weak, the monasteries are declining, and, as Isaiah says, "The grass withereth, the flower fadeth, because the spirit of the Lord bloweth upon it,"‡ through the Gospel. For through the word of God the unchristian and sensual character of these institutions is be-

---

*An adaptation of Isaiah lxii. 1.
† A reference to Luke x. 16.
‡ Isaiah xl. 7.

coming known. And because selfish parents see that they can no longer place their children upon the bounty of monasteries and cathedrals, they refuse to educate them. "Why should we educate our children," they say, "if they are not to become priests, monks, and nuns, and thus earn a support?"

The hollow piety and selfish aims of such persons are sufficiently evident from their own confession. For if they sought anything more than the temporal welfare of their children in monasteries and the priesthood, if they were deeply in earnest to secure the salvation and blessedness of their children, they would not lose interest in education and say, "if the priestly office is abolished, we will not send our children to school." But they would speak after this manner: "if it is true, as the Gospel teaches, that such a calling is dangerous to our children, teach us another way in which they may be pleasing to God and become truly blessed; for we wish to provide not alone for the bodies of our children, but also for their souls." Such would be the language of faithful Christian parents.

It is no wonder that the devil meddles in the matter, and influences groveling hearts to neglect the children and the youth of the country. Who can blame him for it? He is the prince and god of this world,* and with extreme displeasure sees the Gospel destroy his nurseries of vice, the monasteries and priesthood, in which he corrupts the young beyond measure, a work upon which his mind is especially bent. How could he consent to a proper training of the young? Truly he would be a fool if he permitted such a thing in his kingdom, and thus consented to its overthrow: which indeed would happen, if the young should escape him, and be brought up to the service of God.

Hence he acted wisely at the time when Christians were educating and bringing up their children in a Christian way. Inasmuch as the youth of the land would have thus escaped him, and inflicted an irreparable injury upon his kingdom, he went to work and spread his nets, established such monasteries, schools, and orders, that it was not possible for a boy to escape him without the miraculous intervention of God. But now that he sees his snares exposed through the Word of God, he takes an opposite course, and dissuades men from all education whatever. He thus pursues a wise course to maintain his kingdom and win the youth of Germany. And if he secures them, if they grow up under his influence and remain his adherents, who can gain any advantage over him? He

---

*A reference to John xiv. 30.

retains an easy and peaceful mastery over the world. For any fatal wound to his cause must come through the young, who, brought up in the knowledge of God, spread abroad the truth and instruct others.

Yet no one thinks of this dreadful purpose of the devil, which is being worked out so quietly that it escapes observation; and soon the evil will be so far advanced that we can do nothing to prevent it. People fear the Turks, wars, and floods, for in such matters they can see what is injurious or beneficial; but what the devil has in mind no one sees or fears. Yet where we would give a florin to defend ourselves against the Turks, we should give a hundred florins to protect us against ignorance, even if only one boy could be taught to be a truly Christian man; for the good such a man can accomplish is beyond all computation.

Therefore I beg you all, in the name of God and of our neglected youth, not to think of this subject lightly, as many do who see not what the prince of this world intends. For the right instruction of youth is a matter in which Christ and all the world are concerned. Thereby are we all aided. And consider that great Christian zeal is needed to overcome the silent, secret, and artful machinations of the devil. If we must annually expend large sums on muskets, roads, bridges, dams, and the like, in order that the city may have temporal peace and comfort, why should we not apply as much to our poor, neglected youth, in order that we may have a skillful school-master or two?

There is one consideration that should move every citizen, with devout gratitude to God, to contribute a part of his means to the support of schools—the consideration that if divine grace had not released him from exactions and robbery, he would still have to give large sums of money for indulgences, masses, vigils, endowments, anniversaries, mendicant friars, brotherhoods, and other similar impositions. And let him be sure that where turmoil and strife exist, there the devil is present, who did not writhe and struggle so long as men blindly contributed to convents and masses. For Satan feels that his cause is suffering injury. Let this, then, be the first consideration to move you,—that in this work we are fighting against the devil, the most artful and dangerous enemy of men.

Another consideration is found in the fact that we should not, as St. Paul says, receive the grace of God in vain,* and neglect the present favorable time. For Almighty God has truly granted us Germans a gracious visitation, and favored us with a golden oppor-

---
* 2 Cor. vi. 1.

tunity. We now have excellent and learned young men, adorned with every science and art, who, if they were employed, could be of great service as teachers. Is it not well known that a boy can now be so instructed in three years, that at the age of fifteen or eighteen he knows more than all the universities and convents have known heretofore? Yea, what have men learned hitherto in the universities and monasteries, except to be asses and blockheads? Twenty, forty years, it has been necessary to study, and yet one has learned neither Latin nor German! I say nothing of the shameful and vicious life in those institutions, by which our worthy youth have been so lamentably corrupted.

I should prefer, it is true, that our youth be ignorant and dumb rather than that the universities and convents should remain as the only sources of instruction open to them. For it is my earnest intention, prayer and desire that these schools of Satan either be destroyed or changed into Christian schools. But since God has so richly favored us, and given us a great number of persons who are competent thoroughly to instruct and train our young people, it is truly needful that we should not disregard His grace and let Him knock in vain. He stands at the door; happy are we if we open to Him. He calls us; happy is the man who answers Him. If we disregard His call, so that He passes by, who will bring Him back?

Let us consider the wretchedness of our former condition and the darkness in which we were enveloped. I believe Germany has never heard so much of the Word of God as at the present time; history reveals no similar period. If we let the gracious season pass without gratitude and improvement, it is to be feared that we shall suffer still more terrible darkness and distress. My dear countrymen, buy while the market is at your door; gather the harvest while the sun shines and the weather is fair: use the grace and Word of God while they are near. For know this, that the Word and grace of God are like a passing shower, which does not return where it has once been. The Divine favor once rested upon the Jews, but it has departed. Paul brought the Gospel into Greece; but now they have the Turks. Rome and Italy once enjoyed its blessings; but now they have the Pope. And the German people should not think that they will always have it; for ingratitude and neglect will banish it. Therefore seize it and hold it fast, whoever can; idle hands will have an evil year.

The third consideration is the highest of all, namely, God's command, which through Moses so often urges and enjoins that parents instruct their children, that the seventy-eighth Psalm says: "He established a testimony in Jacob and appointed a law in Israel, which he commanded our fathers that they should make them known to their children." And the fourth commandment also shows this, where he has so strictly enjoined children to obey their parents, that disobedient children were to be put to death. And why do old people live, except to care for, teach, and bring up the young? It is not possible for inexperienced youth to instruct and care for themselves; and for that reason God has commended them to us who are older and know what is good for them, and He will require a strict account at our hands. Therefore Moses gives this injunction: "Ask thy father, and he will show thee; thy elders, and they will tell thee." *

It is indeed a sin and shame that we must be aroused and incited to the duty of educating our children and of considering their highest interests, whereas nature itself should move us thereto, and the example of the heathen affords us varied instruction. There is no irrational animal that does not care for and instruct its young in what they should know, except the ostrich, of which God says; "She leaveth her eggs in the earth, and warmeth them in the dust; and is hardened against her young ones, as though they were not

---

*Deut. xxxii. 7.

hers."* And what would it avail if we possessed and performed all else, and became perfect saints, if we neglect that for which we chiefly live, namely, to care for the young? In my judgment there is no other outward offense that in the sight of God so heavily burdens the world, and deserves such heavy chastisement, as the neglect to educate children.

In my youth this proverb was current in the schools: "It is no less a sin to neglect a pupil than to do violence to a woman." It was used to frighten teachers. But how much lighter is this wrong against a woman (which as a bodily sin may be atoned for), than to neglect and dishonor immortal souls, when such a sin is not recognized and can never be atoned for? O eternal woe to the world! Children are daily born and grow up among us, and there are none, alas! who feel an interest in them; and instead of being trained, they are left to themselves. The convents and cathedral schools are the proper agencies to do it; but to them we may apply the words of Christ: "Woe unto the world because of offenses! Whoso shall offend one of these little ones which believe in me, it were better for him that a mill-stone were hanged about his neck, and that he

---

*Job xxxix. 14, 16.

were drowned in the depth of the sea."* They are nothing but destroyers of children.

But all that, you say, is addressed to parents; what does it concern the members of the council and the mayors? That is true; but how, if parents neglect it? Who shall attend to it then? Shall we therefore let it alone, and suffer the children to be neglected? How will the mayors and council excuse themselves, and prove that such a duty does not belong to them?

Parents neglect this duty from various causes.

In the first place, there are some who are so lacking in piety and uprightness that they would not do it if they could, but like the ostrich, harden themselves against their own offspring, and do nothing for them. Nevertheless these children must live among us and with us. How then can reason and, above all, Christian charity, suffer them to grow up ill-bred, and to infect other children, till at last the whole city be destroyed, like Sodom, Gomorrah, and some other cities?

In the second place, the great majority of parents are unqualified for it, and do not uuderstand how children should be brought up and taught. For they have learned nothing but to provide for their bodily wants; and in order to teach and train children thoroughly, a separate class is needed.

---

* Matt. xviii. 6, 7.

In the third place, even if parents were qualified and willing to do it themselves, yet on account of other employments and household duties they have no time for it, so that necessity requires us to have teachers for public schools, unless each parent employ a private instructor. But that would be too expensive for persons of ordinary means, and many a bright boy, on account of poverty, would be neglected. Besides, many parents die and leave orphans; and how they are usually cared for by guardians, we might learn, even if observation were not enough, from the sixty-eighth Psalm, where God calls himself the "Father of the fatherless," as of those who are neglected by all others. Also there are some who have no children, and therefore feel no interest in them.

Therefore it will be the duty of the mayors and council to exercise the greatest care over the young. For since the happiness, honor, and life of the city are committed to their hands, they would be held recreant before God and the world, if they did not, day and night, with all their power, seek its welfare and improvement. Now the welfare of a city does not consist alone in great treasures, firm walls, beautiful houses, and munitions of war; indeed, where all these are found, and reckless fools come into power, the city sustains the greater injury. But the highest welfare, safety, and power of a city consists in able, learned, wise, upright, cultivated citizens, who can secure, preserve, and utilize every treasure and advantage.

In ancient Rome the boys were so brought up that at the age of fifteen, eighteen, twenty, they were masters not only of the choicest Latin and Greek, but also of the liberal arts, as they are called; and immediately after this scholastic training, they entered the army or held a position under the government. Thus they became intelligent, wise, and excellent men, skilled in every art and rich in experience, so that all the bishops, priests, and monks in Germany put together would not equal a Roman soldier. Consequently their country prospered; persons were found capable and skilled in every pursuit. Thus, in all the world, even among the heathen, school-masters and teachers have been found necessary where a nation was to be elevated. Hence in the Epistle to the Galatians Paul employs a word in common use when he says, "The law was our *school-master*."*

Since, then, a city must have well-trained people, and since the greatest need, lack, and lament is that such are not to be found, we must not wait till they grow up of themselves; neither can they be hewed out of stones nor cut out of wood; nor will God work

---

*Gal. iii. 24.

miracles, so long as men can attain their object through means within their reach. Therefore we must see to it, and spare no trouble or expense to educate and form them ourselves. For whose fault is it that in all the cities there are at present so few skillful people except the rulers, who have allowed the young to grow up like trees in the forest, and have not cared how they were reared and taught? The growth, consequently, has been so irregular that the forest furnishes no timber for building purposes, but like a useless hedge, is good only for fuel.

Yet there must be civil government. For us, then, to permit ignoramuses and blockheads to rule when we can prevent it, is irrational and barbarous. Let us rather make rulers out of swine and wolves, and set them over people who are indifferent to the manner in which they are governed. It is barbarous for men to think thus: "We will now rule; and what does it concern us how those fare who shall come after us?" Not over human beings, but over swine and dogs should such people rule, who think only of their own interests and honor in governing. Even if we exercise the greatest care to educate able, learned and skilled rulers, yet much care and effort are necessary in order to secure prosperity. How can a city prosper, when no effort is made?

But, you say again, if we shall and must have schools, what is the use to teach Latin, Greek, Hebrew, and the other liberal arts? Is it not enough to teach the Scriptures, which are necessary to salvation, in the mother tongue? To which I answer: I know, alas! that we Germans must always remain irrational brutes, as we are deservedly called by surrounding nations. But I wonder why we do not also say: of what use to us are silk, wine, spices, and other foreign articles, since we ourselves have an abundance of wine, corn, wool, flax, wood, and stone in the German states, not only for our necessities, but also for embellishment and ornament? The languages and other liberal arts, which are not only harmless, but even a greater ornament, benefit, and honor than these things, both for understanding the Holy Scriptures and carrying on the civil government, we are disposed to despise; and the foreign articles which are neither necessary nor useful, and which besides greatly impoverish us, we are unwilling to dispense with. Are we not rightly called German dunces and brutes?

Indeed, if the languages were of no practical benefit, we ought still to feel an interest in them as a wonderful gift of God, with which he has now blessed Germany almost beyond all other lands. We do not find many instances in which Satan has fostered them through the universities and cloisters; on the contrary, these institutions have fiercely inveighed and continue to inveigh against them. For the devil scented the danger that would threaten his kingdom, if the languages should be generally studied. But since he could not wholly prevent their cultivation, he aims at least to confine them within such narrow limits, that they will of themselves decline and fall into disuse. They are to him no welcome guest, and consequently he shows them scant courtesy in order that they may not remain long. This malicious trick of Satan is perceived by very few.

Therefore, my beloved countrymen, let us open our eyes, thank God for this precious treasure, and take pains to preserve it, and to frustrate the design of Satan. For we cannot deny that, although the Gospel has come and daily comes through the Holy Spirit, it has come by means of the languages, and through them must increase and be preserved. For when God wished through the apostles to spread the Gospel abroad in all the world, he gave the languages for that purpose; and by means of the Roman empire he made Latin and Greek the language of many lands, that his Gospel might speedily bear fruit far and wide. He has done the same now. For a time no one understood why God had revived the study of the languages; but now we see that it was for the sake of the Gospel, which he wished to bring to light and thereby expose and destroy the reign of Antichrist. For the same reason he gave Greece a prey to the Turks, in order that Greek scholars, driven from home and scattered abroad, might bear the Greek tongue to other countries, and thereby excite an interest in the study of languages.

In the same measure that the Gospel is dear to us, should we zealously cherish the languages. For God had a purpose in giving the Scriptures only in two languages, the Old Testament in the Hebrew, and the New Testament in the Greek. What God did not despise, but chose before all others for His Word, we should likewise esteem above all others. St. Paul, in the third chapter of Romans, points out, as a special honor and advantage of the Hebrew language, that God's Word was given in it: "What profit is there of circumcision? Much every way; chiefly because that unto them were committed the oracles of God." *
Likewise King David boasts in the one hundred and forty-seventh Psalm: "He showeth his word unto Jacob, his statutes and his judgments unto Israel. He hath not dealt so with any nation: and as for his

---

* Rom. iii. 1, 2.

judgments, they have not known them." * Hence the Hebrew language is called sacred. And St. Paul, in Romans i. 2, speaks of the Hebrew Scriptures as holy, no doubt because of the Word of God which they contain. In like manner the Greek language might well be called holy, because it was chosen, in preference to others, as the language of the New Testament. And from this language, as from a fountain, the New Testament has flowed through translations into other languages, and sanctified them also.

And let this be kept in mind, that we will not preserve the Gospel without the languages. The languages are the scabbard in which the Word of God is sheathed. They are the casket in which this jewel is enshrined; the cask in which this wine is kept; the chamber in which this food is stored. And, to borrow a figure from the Gospel itself, they are the baskets in which this bread, and fish, and fragments are preserved. If through neglect we lose the languages (which may God forbid), we will not only lose the Gospel, but it will finally come to pass that we will lose also the ability to speak and write either Latin or German. Of this let us take as proof and warning the miserable and shocking example presented in the universities and cloisters, in which not only the Gospel has been per-

---

*Psalm cxlvii. 19, 20.

verted, but also the Latin and German languages have been corrupted, so that the wretched inmates have become like brutes, unable to speak and write German or Latin, and have almost lost their natural reason.

The apostles considered it necessary to embody the New Testament in the Greek language, in order, no doubt, that it might be securely preserved unto us as in a sacred shrine. For they foresaw what has since taken place, namely, that when the divine revelation is left to oral tradition, much disorder and confusion arise from conflicting opinions and doctrines. And there would be no way to prevent this evil and to protect the simple-minded, if the New Testament was not definitely recorded in writing. Therefore it is evident that where the languages are not preserved, there the Gospel will become corrupted.

Experience shows this to be true. For immediately after the age of the apostles, when the languages ceased to be cultivated, the Gospel, and the true faith, and Christianity itself, declined more and more, until they were entirely lost under the Pope. And since the time that the languages disappeared, not much that is noteworthy and excellent has been seen in the Church; but through ignorance of the languages very many shocking abominations have arisen. On the other hand, since the revival of learning, such a light has been shed abroad, and such important changes have taken place, that the world is astonished, and must acknowledge that we have the Gospel almost as pure and unadulterated as it was in the times of the apostles, and much purer than it was in the days of St. Jerome and St. Augustine. In a word, since the Holy Ghost, who does nothing foolish or useless, has often bestowed the gift of tongues, it is our evident duty earnestly to cultivate the languages, now that God has restored them to the world through the revival of learning.

But many of the church fathers, you say, have become saints and have taught without a knowledge of the languages. That is true. But to what do you attribute their frequent misunderstanding of the Scriptures? How often is St. Augustine in error in the Psalms and in other expositions, as well as Hilary, and indeed all those who have undertaken to explain the Scriptures without an acquaintance with the original tongues? And if perchance they have taught correct doctrine, they have not been sure of the application to be made of particular passages. For example, it is truly said that Christ is the Son of God. But what mockery does it seem to adversaries when as proof of that doctrine Psalm cx. 3 is adduced: "*Tecum principium in die virtutis,*" since in the

Hebrew no reference is made in that verse to the Deity. When the faith is thus defended with uncertain reasons and proof-texts, does it not seem a disgrace and mockery in the eyes of such adversaries as are acquainted with the Greek and the Hebrew? And they are only rendered the more obstinate in their error, and with good ground hold our faith as a human delusion.

What is the reason that our faith is thus brought into disgrace? It is our ignorance of the languages; and the only remedy is a knowledge of them. Was not St. Jerome forced to make a new translation of the Psalms from the Hebrew, because the Jews, when quotations were made from the Latin version, derided the Christians, affirming that the passages adduced were not found in the original? The comments of all the ancient fathers who, without a knowledge of the languages, have treated of the Scriptures (although they may teach nothing heretical), are still of such a character that the writers often employ uncertain, doubtful, and inappropriate expressions, and grope like a blind man along a wall, so that they often miss the sense of the text and mould it according to their pious fancy, as in the example mentioned in the last paragraph. St. Augustine himself was obliged to confess that the Christian teacher, in addition to Latin, should be acquainted with Hebrew and Greek. Without this knowledge, the expositor will inevitably fall into mistakes; and even when the languages are understood, he will meet with difficulties.

With a simple preacher of the faith it is different from what it is with the expositor of the Scriptures, or prophet, as St. Paul calls him. The former has so many clear passages and texts in translations, that he is able to understand and preach Christ, and lead a holy life. But to explain the Scriptures, to deal with them independently, and oppose heretical interpreters, such a one is too weak without a knowledge of the languages. But we need just such expositors, who will give themselves to the study and interpretation of the Scriptures, and who are able to controvert erroneous doctrines; for a pious life and orthodox teaching are not alone sufficient. Therefore the languages are absolutely necessary, as well as prophets or expositors; but it is not necessary that every Christian or preacher be such a prophet, according to the diversity of gifts of which St. Paul speaks in 1 Corinthians xii. 8, 9, and in Ephesians iv. 11.

This explains why, since the days of the apostles, the Scriptures have remained in obscurity, and no reliable and enduring expositions have anywhere been written. For even the holy fathers, as we have said, are often in error, and because they were not versed in the languages, they seldom agree. St. Bernard was a man of great ability, so that I am inclined to place him above all other distinguished teachers, whether ancient or modern; but how often he trifles with the Scriptures, in a spiritual manner to be sure, and wrests them from their true meaning! For the same reason the Papists have said that the Scriptures are of obscure and peculiar import. But they do not perceive that the trouble lies in ignorance of the languages; but for this, nothing simpler has ever been spoken than the Word of God. A Turk must indeed speak unintelligibly to me, although a Turkish child of seven years understands him, because I am unacquainted with the language.

Hence it is foolish to attempt to learn the Scriptures through the comments of the fathers and the study of many books and glosses. For that purpose we ought to give ourselves to the languages. For the beloved fathers, because they were not versed in the languages, have often failed, in spite of their verbose expositions, to give the meaning of the text. You peruse their writings with great toil; and yet with a knowledge of the languages you can get the meaning of Scripture better than they do. For in comparison with the glosses of the fathers, the languages are as sunlight to darkness.

Since, then, it behooves Christians at all times to use the Bible as their only book and to be thoroughly acquainted with it, especially is it a disgrace and sin at the present day not to learn the languages, when God provides every facility, incites us to study, and wishes to have His word known. O how glad the honored fathers would have been, if they could have learned the languages, and had such access to the Holy Scriptures! With what pain and toil they scarcely obtained crumbs, while almost without effort we are able to secure the whole loaf! O how their industry shames our idleness, yea, how severely will God punish our neglect and ingratitude!

St. Paul, in 1. Corinthians xiv. 29,* enjoins that there be judgment upon doctrine—a duty that requires a knowledge of the languages. For the preacher or teacher may publicly read the whole Bible as he chooses, right or wrong, if there be no one present to judge whether he does it correctly or not. But if one is to judge, there must be an acquaintance with the languages; otherwise, the judging will be in vain. Hence, although faith and the Gospel may be preached by ordinary ministers without the languages, still such preaching is sluggish and

---

*Let the prophets speak two or three, and let the other judge.

weak, and the people finally become weary, and fall away. But a knowledge of the languages renders it lively and strong, and faith finds itself constantly renewed through rich and varied instruction. In the first Psalm the Scriptures liken such study to "a tree planted by the rivers of water, that bringeth forth its fruit in its season; its leaf also shall not wither."

We should not allow ourselves to be deceived because there are some who, while setting little store by the Scriptures, boast of the Spirit. Some also, like the Waldenses, do not regard the languages useful. But, dear friend, whatever such persons may say, I have also been in the Spirit, and have seen more of His power (if it is allowable to boast of one's self), than they will see in a year, however much they may vaunt themselves. I have also been able to accomplish somewhat, while they have remained without influence, and done little more than boast. I know full well that the Spirit does almost everything. Still I should have failed in my work, if the languages had not come to my aid, and made me strong and immovable in the Scriptures. I might without them have been pious, and preached the Gospel in obscurity; but I could not have disturbed the Pope, his adherents, and all the reign of Antichrist. The devil cares less for the Spirit within me than for my pen and linguistic knowledge. For while the Spirit takes nothing but myself away from him, the Holy Scriptures and the languages drive him from the world and break up his kingdom.

I can not praise the Waldenses for depreciating the languages. For although they taught no heresies, yet they often necessarily failed in their proof-texts, and remained unqualified and unskilled to contend against error for the true faith. Besides, their teaching is so unenlightened, and presented in such peculiar forms, not following the language of Scripture, that I fear it will not continue pure. For it is dangerous to speak of divine things in a manner or in words different from those employed in the Scriptures. In brief, they may lead holy lives and teach among themselves; but because they are without the languages, they will lack what others have lacked, namely, an assured and thorough handling of the Scriptures, and the ability to be useful to other nations. And because they could have done this, and would not, they will have an account to render before God for their neglect.

So much for the utility and necessity of the languages, and of Christian schools for our spiritual interests and the salvation of the soul. Let us now consider the body and inquire: though there were no soul, nor heaven, nor hell, but only the civil government, would not this require good schools and learned men more than do our spiritual interests? Hitherto the Papists have taken no interest in civil government, and have conducted the schools so entirely in the interests of the priesthood, that it has become a matter of reproach for a learned man to marry, and he has been forced to hear remarks like this: "Behold, he has become a man of the world, and cares nothing for the clerical state," just as if the priestly order were alone acceptable to God, and the secular classes, as they are called, belonged to Satan, and were unchristian. But in the sight of God, the former rather belong to Satan, while the despised masses (as happened to the people of Israel in the Babylonian captivity) remain in the land and in right relations with God.

It is not necessary to say here that civil government is a divine institution; of that I have elsewhere said so much, that I hope no one has any doubts on the subject. The question is, how are we to get able and skillful rulers? And here we are put to shame by the heathen, who in ancient times, especially the Greeks and Romans, without knowing that civil government is a divine ordinance, yet instructed the boys and girls with such earnestness and industry that, when I think of it, I am ashamed of Christians, and especially of our

Germans, who are such blockheads and brutes that they can say: "Pray, what is the use of schools, if one is not to become a priest?" Yet we know, or ought to know, how necessary and useful a thing it is, and how acceptable to God, when a prince, lord, counsellor, or other ruler, is well-trained and skillful in discharging, in a Christian way, the functions of his office.

Even if there were no soul, (as I have already said,) and men did not need schools and the languages for the sake of Christianity and the Scriptures, still, for the establishment of the best schools everywhere, both for boys and girls, this consideration is of itself sufficient, namely, that society, for the maintenance of civil order and the proper regulation of the household, needs accomplished and well-trained men and women. Now such men are to come from boys, and such women from girls; hence it is necessary that boys and girls be properly taught and brought up. As I have before said, the ordinary man is not qualified for this task, and can not, and will not do it. Princes and lords ought to do it; but they spend their time in pleasure-driving, drinking, and folly, and are burdened with the weighty duties of the cellar, kitchen and bedchamber. And though some would be glad to do it, they must stand in fear of the rest, lest they be taken for fools or heretics. Therefore, honored members of the city councils, this work must remain in your hands; you have more time and better opportunity for it than princes and lords.

But each one, you say, may educate and discipline his own sons and daughters. To which I reply: We see indeed how it goes with this teaching and training. And where it is carried to the highest point, and is attended with success, it results in nothing more than that the learners, in some measure, acquire a forced external propriety of manner; in other respects they remain dunces, knowing nothing, and incapable of giving aid or advice. But were they instructed in schools or elsewhere by thoroughly qualified male or female teachers, who taught the languages, other arts, and history, then the pupils would hear the history and maxims of the world, and see how things went with each city, kingdom, prince, man, and woman; and thus, in a short time, they would be able to comprehend, as in a mirror, the character, life, counsels, undertakings, successes, and failures, of the whole world from the beginning. From this knowledge they could regulate their views, and order their course of life in the fear of God, having become wise in judging what is to be sought and what avoided in this outward life, and capable of advising and directing others.

But the training which is given at home is expected to make us wise through our own experience. Before that can take place, we shall die a hundred times, and all through life act injudiciously; for much time is needed to give experience.

Now since the young must leap and jump, or have something to do, because they have a natural desire for it which should not be restrained, (for it is not well to check them in everything,) why should we not provide for them such schools, and lay before them such studies? By the gracious arrangement of God, children take delight in acquiring knowledge, whether languages, mathematics, or history. And our schools are no longer a hell or purgatory, in which children are tortured over cases and tenses, and in which with much flogging, trembling, anguish and wretchedness they learn nothing. If we take so much time and pains to teach our children to play cards, sing, and dance, why should we not take as much time to teach them reading and other branches of knowledge, while they are young and at leisure, are quick at learning, and take delight in it? As for myself,* if I had children and were able, I would have them learn not only the languages and history, but also singing, instrumental music, and the whole course of mathematics. For

---

* Luther was not yet married.

what is all this but mere child's play, in which the Greeks in former ages trained their children, and by this means became wonderfully skillful people, capable for every undertaking? How I regret that I did not read more poetry and history, and that no one taught me in these branches. Instead of these I was obliged with great cost, labor, and injury, to read Satanic filth, the Aristotelian and Scholastic philosophy, so that I have enough to do to get rid of it.

But you say, who can do without his children and bring them up, in this manner, to be young gentlemen? I reply: it is not my idea that we should establish schools as they have been heretofore, where a boy has studied Donatus and Alexander* twenty or thirty years, and yet has learned nothing. The world has changed, and things go differently. My idea is that boys should spend an hour or two a day in school, and the rest of the time work at home, learn some trade and do whatever is desired, so that study and work may go on together, while the children are young and can attend to both. They now spend tenfold as much time in shooting with crossbows, playing ball, running, and tumbling about.

---

*Donatus wrote a Latin grammar used as a text-book during the Middle Ages. Alexander was the author of a commentary on Aristotle.

In like manner, a girl has time to go to school an hour a day, and yet attend to her work at home; for she sleeps, dances, and plays away more than that. The real difficulty is found alone in the absence of an earnest desire to educate the young, and to aid and benefit mankind with accomplished citizens. The devil much prefers blockheads and drones, that men may have more abundant trials and sorrows in the world.

But the brightest pupils, who give promise of becoming accomplished teachers, preachers, and workers, should be kept longer at school, or set apart wholly for study, as we read of the holy martyrs, who brought up St. Agnes, St. Agatha, St. Lucian, and others. For this purpose also the cloisters and cathedral schools were founded, but they have been perverted into another and accursed use. There is great need for such instruction; for the tonsured crowd is rapidly decreasing, and besides, for the most part, the monks are unskilled to teach and rule, since they know nothing but to care for their stomachs, the only thing they have been taught. Hence we must have persons qualified to dispense the Word of God and the Sacraments, and to be pastors of the people. But where will we obtain them, if schools are not established on a more Christian basis, since those hitherto maintained, even if they do not go down, can produce nothing but depraved and dangerous corrupters of youth?

There is consequently an urgent necessity, not only for the sake of the young, but also for the maintenance of Christianity and of civil government, that this matter be immediately and earnestly taken hold of, lest afterwards, although we would gladly attend to it, we shall find it impossible to do so, and be obliged to feel in vain the pangs of remorse forever. For God is now graciously present, and offers his aid. If we despise it, we already have our condemnation with the people of Israel, of whom Isaiah says: "I have spread out my hands all the day unto a rebellious people."* And Proverbs i. 24–26: "I have stretched out my hand, and no man regarded: but ye have set at naught all my counsel, and would none of my reproof: I also will laugh at your calamity; I will mock when your fear cometh." Let us then take heed. Consider for example what great zeal Solomon manifested; for he was so much interested in the young that he took time, in the midst of his imperial duties, to write a book for them called Proverbs. And think how Christ himself took the little children in His arms! How earnestly He commends them to

---

*Isaiah lxv. 2.

us, and speaks of their guardian angels,* in order that He may show us how great a service it is, when we rightly bring them up: on the other hand, how His anger kindles, if we offend the little ones, and let them perish.

Therefore, dear Sirs, take to heart this work, which God so urgently requires at your hands, which pertains to your office, which is necessary for the young, and which neither the world nor the Spirit can do without. We have, alas! lived and degenerated long enough in darkness; we have remained German brutes too long. Let us use our reason, that God may observe in us gratitude for His mercies, and that other lands may see that we are human beings, capable both of learning and of teaching, in order that through us, also, the world may be made better. I have done my part; I have desired to benefit the German states, although some have despised me and set my counsel at naught as knowing better themselves,—to all which I must submit. I know indeed that others could have accomplished it better; but because they were silent, I have done the best I could. It is better to have spoken, even though imperfectly, than to have remained silent. And I have hope that God will rouse some of you to listen to my counsel, and that

---

*Matt. xviii. 10.

instead of considering the adviser, you will let yourselves be moved by the great interests at stake.

Finally, this must be taken into consideration by all who earnestly desire to see such schools established and the languages preserved in the German states: that no cost nor pains should be spared to procure good libraries in suitable buildings, especially in the large cities, which are able to afford it. For if a knowledge of the Gospel and of every kind of learning is to be preserved, it must be embodied in books, as the prophets and apostles did, as I have already shown. This should be done, not only that our spiritual and civil leaders may have something to read and study, but also that good books may not be lost, and that the arts and languages may be preserved, with which God has graciously favored us. St. Paul was diligent in this matter, since he lays the injunction upon Timothy: "Give attendance to reading;"* and directs him to bring the books, but especially the parchments left at Troas.†

All the kingdoms that have been distinguished in the world have bestowed care upon this matter, and particularly the Israelites, among whom Moses was the first to begin the work, who commanded them to

---
* 1 Tim. iv. 13.
† 2 Tim. iv. 13.

preserve the book of the law in the ark of God, and put it under the care of the Levites, that any one might procure copies from them. He even commanded the king to make a copy of this book in the hands of the Levites. Among other duties, God directed the Levitical priesthood to preserve and attend to the books. Afterwards Joshua increased and improved this library, as did subsequently Samuel, David, Solomon, Isaiah, and many kings and prophets. Hence have come to us the Holy Scriptures of the Old Testament, which would not otherwise have been collected and preserved, if God had not required such diligence in regard to it.

After this example the collegiate churches and convents formerly founded libraries, although with few good books. And the injury resulting from the neglect to procure books and good libraries, when there were men and books enough for that purpose, was afterwards perceived in the decline of every kind of knowledge; and instead of good books, the senseless, useless, and hurtful books of the monks, the Catholicon, Florista, Graecista, Labyrinthus, Dormi Secure,* and the like were introduced by Satan, so that the Latin language was corrupted, and neither good schools, good instruction, nor good methods of

---

*Names of Latin grammars and collections of sermons.

study remained. And as we see, the languages and arts are, in an imperfect manner, recovered from fragments of old books rescued from the worms and dust; and every day men are seeking these literary remains, as people dig in the ashes of a ruined city after treasures and jewels.

Therein we have received our just due, and God has well recompensed our ingratitude, in that we did not consider His benefits, and lay up a supply of good literature when we had time and opportunity, but neglected it, as if we were not concerned. He in turn, instead of the Holy Scriptures and good books, suffered Aristotle and numberless pernicious books to come into use, which only led us further from the Bible. To these were added the progeny of Satan, the monks and the phantoms of the universities, which we founded at incredible cost, and many doctors, preachers, teachers, priests and monks, that is to say, great, coarse, fat asses, adorned with red and brown caps, like swine led with a golden chain and decorated with pearls; and we have burdened ourselves with them, who have taught us nothing useful, but have made us more and more blind and stupid, and as a reward have consumed all our property, and filled all the cloisters, and indeed every corner, with the dregs and filth of their unclean and noxious books, of which we can not think without horror.

Has it not been a grievous misfortune that a boy has hitherto been obliged to study twenty years or longer, in order to learn enough miserable Latin to become a priest and to read the mass? And whoever has succeeded in this, has been called blessed, and blessed the mother that has borne such a child! And yet he has remained a poor ignorant man all through life, and has been of no real service whatever. Everywhere we have had such teachers and masters, who have known nothing themselves, who have been able to teach nothing useful, and who have been ignorant even of the right methods of learning and teaching. How has it come about? No books have been accessible but the senseless trash of the monks and sophists. How could the pupils and teachers differ from the books they studied? A jackdaw does not hatch a dove, nor a fool make a man wise. That is the recompense of our ingratitude, in that we did not use diligence in the formation of libraries, but allowed good books to perish, and bad ones to survive.

But my advice is, not to collect all sorts of books indiscriminately, thinking only of getting a vast number together. I would have discrimination used, because it is not necessary to collect the commentaries of all the jurists, the productions of all the theologians, the discussions of all the philosophers, and the sermons of all the monks. Such trash I would reject altogether, and provide my library only with useful books; and in making the selection, I would advise with learned men.

In the first place, a library should contain the Holy Scriptures in Latin, Greek, Hebrew, German, and other languages. Then the best and most ancient commentators in Greek, Hebrew, and Latin.

Secondly, such books as are useful in acquiring the languages, as the poets and orators, without considering whether they are heathen or Christian, Greek or Latin. For it is from such works that grammar must be learned.

Thirdly, books treating of all the arts and sciences.

Lastly, books on jurisprudence and medicine, though here discrimination is necessary.

A prominent place should be given to chronicles and histories, in whatever languages they may be obtained; for they are wonderfully useful in understanding and regulating the course of the world, and in disclosing the marvelous works of God. O how many noble deeds and wise maxims produced on German soil have been forgotten and lost, because no one at the time wrote them down; or if they were written, no one preserved the books: hence we Germans are unknown in other lands, and are called brutes that know only how to fight, eat, and drink. But the Greeks and Romans, and even the Hebrews, have recorded their history with such particularity, that even if a woman or child did any thing noteworthy, all the world was obliged to read and know it; but we Germans are always Germans, and will remain Germans.

Since God has so graciously and abundantly provided us with art, scholars, and books, it is time for us to reap the harvest and gather for future use the treasures of these golden years. For it is to be feared, (and even now it is beginning to take place,) that new and different books will be produced, until at last, through the agency of the devil, the good books which are being printed will be crowded out by the multitude of ill-considered, senseless, and noxious works. For Satan certainly designs that we should torture ourselves again with Catholicons, Floristas, Modernists, and other trash of the accursed monks and sophists, always learning, yet never acquiring knowledge.

Therefore, my dear Sirs, I beg you to let my labor bear fruit with you. And though there be some who think me too insignificant to follow my advice, or who look down upon me as one condemned by tyrants: still let them consider that I am not seeking my own interest, but that of all Germany. And even if I were a fool, and should yet hit upon something good, no wise man should think it a disgrace to follow me. And even if I were a Turk and heathen, and it should yet appear that my advice was advantageous, not for myself, but for Christianity, no reasonable person would despise my counsel. Sometimes a fool has given better advice than a whole company of wise men. Moses received instruction from Jethro.

Herewith I commend you all to the grace of God. May He soften your hearts, and kindle therein a deep interest in behalf of the poor, wretched, and neglected youth; and through the blessing of God may you so counsel and aid them as to attain to a happy Christian social order in respect to both body and soul, with all fullness and abounding plenty, to the praise and honor of God the Father, through Jesus Christ our Saviour. Amen.

Wittenberg, 1524.

CHAPTER X.

SERMON ON THE DUTY OF SENDING CHILDREN TO SCHOOL.

DEDICATORY LETTER.

To the Honorable Lazarus Spengler, Counselor of the City of Nuremberg,

My dear Sir and Friend: Grace and peace in Christ, our dear Lord and faithful Saviour, Amen.

I have prepared a sermon to the preachers, who are scattered here and there, on the duty of admonishing their people to send their children to school; and it has so grown on my hands as to become in fact a book, though I have been obliged to restrain myself lest it become too large, so rich and fruitful is the subject. Desiring that it might accomplish much good, I have sent it forth under your name, with no other purpose than that it might thereby attract more attention, and be read, if it is worthy, among your citizens. For, although I can well believe that your preachers are active enough, and that they, as highly favored of God, recognize and further this interest, so that—thanks be to God—they do not need my admonition and instruction; yet it does no harm that many agree in this matter, and thus present a stronger front to the devil.

For in such a great city and among so many citizens, the devil will certainly try his art and tempt some to despise the Word of God; and in particular, since commerce and trade will present many occasions for it, he will seek to turn the children from education to the service of Mammon. No doubt this is now occupying his thoughts; for if he should succeed in having the Word and schools neglected in Nuremberg, he would have accomplished a great task, since he would have set an example that would have much weight in all Germany, and deal a heavy blow to education in other cities. For Nuremberg truly shines in Germany as a sun among the moon and stars, and powerfully influences the life of other communities.

But thanks and praises be to God, who long ago anticipated the devil's thoughts and caused your honorable Council to establish such an excellent school that without boasting I may say that no other university, not even that of Paris, has been better provided with teachers, as all must testify who are acquainted with such institutions. For my part I am acquainted with them only too well! But that institution is an ornament to your city, and is widely celebrated, like the wise Council who, in its establishment, showed a Christian regard for their subjects, and provided, not only for their eternal weal, but also for their temporal needs and honor. Which work God will certainly continue to strengthen more and more with His blessing and grace, though the devil struggle against it for a time; for he can not see with pleasure that such a tabernacle be built to our God in this sun among cities, and he collects clouds, mists, and dust, so that its splendor may be obscured and darkened. And how could he do otherwise?

Accordingly I hope that the citizens will recognize the fidelity and love of such Councillors, and help earnestly to strengthen the work by keeping their children at school, since they see that without cost to themselves their children have been richly and assiduously provided for. Especially should the preachers urge it; for where they do not do so, the ordinary man is tempted and deceived by Satan, so that he easily loses sight of his duty, and fails to realize, by reason of his manifold employments, the benefits and injury at stake. Therefore we should exercise patience, when the people are not obdurate and wicked. For I know that Nuremberg has many citizens who, God be thanked, gladly do their duty when they recognize or are taught it—a glory they have not only with me, but also throughout Germany.

DUTY OF SENDING CHILDREN TO SCHOOL. 213

But it will not fail that some worshiper of Mammon will withdraw his son from school and say that "a knowledge of arithmetic and reading is enough, since we now have German books, etc.," and thus set a bad example before pious citizens, who follow him to their injury, in the opinion that he has done well. In this matter preachers can be of service. For a congregation, and especially a large city must have not only merchants, but also people who know more than arithmetic and reading in German books. German books are made especially for the common man to read at home. But for preaching, governing, and directing, both in the spiritual and the secular sphere, all the sciences and languages of the world are insufficient, let alone the German, particularly at this time when we have to speak with more people than neighbor Jack. But these devotees of Mammon do not think of government, nor consider that without preaching and ruling they would not be able to serve their idol for an hour.

I must believe that among so many people there are a few who do not care about the honor or shame of the excellent city of Nuremberg, so they get their penny. But we should pay no attention to such hurtful Mammon worshipers, but consider that, as it is a high honor for such a city to have an honorable Council providing faithfully for schools, so it would be a great shame for the citizens to despise the fidelity of their rulers, and thus make themselves participators in the bad example and scandal that would be set before other cities, which might afterwards say, "That is the way they do at Nuremburg: why should we do better?"

But if you idolaters will not consider what is godly and honorable, and will think only of Mammon, God will find others to do His work. For I have known cities, thanks be to God, in which, when the Council showed itself indifferent to schools, the pious citizens took the matter in hand and compelled the Council to establish schools and provide ministers. In like manner at Nuremberg, if God wills, the shame of your evil example will not be permitted to influence the people to despise the schools, which an honorable Council, with great fidelity and expense, has established.

But whither, my dear friend, am I running with my letter? It is one of those things which a person can say a great deal about; but I wish herewith, in your name, to speak to all your citizens, and I beg you not to think evil of me; but, as you have hitherto done, to help forward the cause. God knows I mean well. May Christ our Lord strengthen and preserve you against that day, when if God will, we shall with joy behold each other in another form. For He who has hitherto enabled you to do so much in His work and Word, will continue and finish it, to whom be praise and thanksgiving forever. Amen.

Your obedient,   MARTIN LUTHER.

Wittenberg, 1530.

———

To all Pastors and Preachers, my dear Friends, who love Christ in sincerity.   MARTIN LUTHER.
Grace and peace in Christ Jesus our Lord.

My very dear Sirs and Friends: You see plainly how Satan is now attacking us on all sides, both with power and cunning, and brings about every misery, that he may destroy the holy Gospel and the kingdom of God, or, if he can not destroy it, that he may at least hinder it in every way, and prevent its progress and success. Among his various crafty devices, one of the greatest, if not the greatest, is to delude the common people into withholding their children from school and instruction, while he suggests to them such hurtful thoughts as these: "Since there is no hope for the cloisters and priesthood as formerly, we do not need learned men and study, but must consider how we may obtain food and wealth."

That is a master-piece of Satanic art; since he sees that he can not have his way in our times, he thinks to accomplish his purpose with our descendants, whom before our eyes he seeks to withhold from learning and knowledge. And thus, when we are dead, he will have a naked and defenseless people before him, with whom he can do as he pleases. For if the Scriptures and learning perish, what will remain in Germany, but a lawless horde of Tartars or Turks, yea, a multitude of wild beasts? Such results he does not allow to appear at present, and powerfully blinds the people, that when the evil does come, and they are obliged to learn it from experience, he may laugh at their misery and lamentation, which they can no longer do any thing to help. They will then be forced to say, "We have waited too long," and would give a hundred florins for half a scholar, while now they would not give five florins for a thorough one.

And because they are not willing now to support and keep pious, honorable, and skillful school-masters and teachers who at small expense and with great industry and pains would educate their children in the fear of God, in science, doctrine, and honor, it would almost serve them right to have again, as in former times, a set of ignorant and unprincipled pedagogues who at great cost would teach their children nothing but to be blockheads, and who besides would dishonor their wives, daughters, and maid-servants. Such will be the reward of their great, shameful ingratitude, into which the devil so cunningly leads them.

Since now as pastors we are to watch against these and other wicked devices, we must not sleep, but advise, urge, and admonish, with all might, industry, and care, that the common people may not allow themselves to be deceived and led astray by the devil. Therefore let every one take heed to himself and to his office that he may not sleep and thus let the devil become god and lord; for if we are silent and sleep, so that the youth are neglected and our descendants become Tartars or wild beasts, we will have to bear the responsibility and render a heavy account.

Although I know that many of you, without my admonition, attend to this matter faithfully (in reference to which I formerly addressed a special treatise to the Mayors and Aldermen of the German cities), yet, if some perchance forget it, or wish to follow my example in laboring at it more diligently, I send you this sermon, which I have more than once delivered to our people here, that you may see that I strive earnestly with you, and that we thus everywhere do our duty and in our office are justified before God. Much depends truly upon us, since we see that some who are even called ministers, go about the matter as if they wished to let all schools, discipline, and doctrine perish, or even to help to destroy them, since they cannot, as hitherto, lead the wanton life to which Satan impels them. God help us, Amen.

THE SERMON.

Inasmuch as I see, dear friends, that the common people are placing themselves in opposition to the schools, and that they wish to bring up their children without other instruction than that pertaining to their bodily wants; and inasmuch also as they do not consider what a fearful and unchristian course they are thus pursuing, and what a great and murderous injury they are inflicting, in the service of Satan, upon society, I have undertaken to address you this admonition, in the hope that perchance there are some who yet in some measure at least believe that there is a God in heaven, and a hell ready for the wicked (for all the world acts just as if there were neither a God in heaven nor devils in hell), and in the hope also that there are some who will heed the admonition after comtemplating the advantages and disadvantages of education.

We will first consider the subject in its spiritual or eternal aspects, and afterward in its temporal or secular relations. I trust that believers and all who wish to be called Christians understand that the ministerial office was instituted of God, not with gold and silver, but with the precious blood and bitter death of his only Son, our Lord Jesus Christ. For from His wounds, (as is shown in the epistles) truly flow the sacraments, and His blood has dearly purchased for mankind the blessing of the ministerial office, the function of which is to preach, baptize, loose, bind, dispense the sacraments, comfort, warn, admonish with God's Word, and do whatever else pertains to the care of souls. Such an office not only promotes temporal life and every secular condition, but it also gives eternal life, releases from death and sin, which is its peculiar and distinguished work; and indeed the world stands and abides only on account of this office, without which it would long since have perished.

But I do not mean the clerical office, with its celibate manner of life, as seen in the cloisters and cathedrals; for it has there degenerated from its original excellent purpose, and become a device for obtaining money and contributions from the people; it has nothing clerical about it but celibacy, which is not necessary, and it consists alone in external, worldly display; for the Word of God and the work of preaching are totally disregarded. Where the Scriptures are neglected, there the clergy must be worthless.

But I mean the clerical office which pays attention

to preaching and the ministration of the Word and Sacraments; which imparts the Holy Spirit and salvation—blessings not to be obtained by means of music and display; which includes the duties of pastor, teacher, preacher, reader, chaplain, sexton, and schoolmaster; and which is highly praised and extolled in the Scriptures. St. Paul speaks of ministers as the stewards and servants of God, bishops, prophets, and also ambassadors of God to reconcile the world to God (2 Cor. v. 20). Joel calls them the Lord's messengers; David calls them kings and princes; Haggai calls them messengers; and Malachi says, "The priest's lips should keep knowledge; for he is the messenger of the Lord of hosts" (Mal. ii. 7); as Christ also says, Matthew xi. 10, when he calls John the Baptist a messenger, and also throughout the book of Revelation.

The ancients were very loth to assume this office on account of its great worth and responsibility, and they had to be urged and forced to do so; but afterwards, and up to the present time, there have been many who have praised the office on account of the mass more than on account of preaching, which praise has increased to such a point that the priests are exalted above Mary and the angels, because the angels and Mary cannot celebrate mass. A new priest and a first mass have been held of great importance, and blessed has been the mother that has borne a priest; but the Word of God and the work of preaching, which is the highest function of the clerical office, have been disregarded. And in a word, a man who could celebrate mass, has been called a priest, although he has not been able to preach at all, and has been only an unlearned ass; and such for the most part is the clerical office to-day.

If it is certain and true that God has instituted the office of the ministry with His own blood and death, we may be sure that He desires to have it highly honored, and continued till the day of judgment. For the Gospel and Christianity must abide till that day, as Christ says, Matthew xxviii. 20: "Lo, I am with you alway, even unto the end." But through whom is it to be continued? Oxen and horses, dogs and swine, will not do it, nor wood and stone; it must be done by men: for this office has not been committed to oxen and horses, but to men. But where shall we find persons for this work, except among those who have children? If you refuse to bring up your child for it, and others do the same, so that no fathers and mothers give their children to our God, how can the ministerial office be filled? The present incumbents can not live forever, but are dying daily; and if there are none to take their places, what will God say? Do you suppose it will be pleasing to Him that an office, divinely instituted for His honor and glory, and our salvation, is shamefully despised and with base ingratitude allowed to perish?

He has given the children and the means of their support, not that you might simply have pleasure in them and bring them up for worldly display. You are earnestly commanded to bring them up for the service of God; and otherwise you will perish with your children, as the First Commandment says: "I the Lord thy God am a jealous God, visiting the iniquity of the fathers upon the children unto the third and fourth generation of them that hate me." *

But how will you bring them up to the service of God when preaching and the ministerial office have passed away? And the fault is yours, since you might have helped to preserve them, if you had instructed your child. For when you can teach your child, and it is capable and desirous of learning, and you do not aid but hinder it, (mark my words well!) you are responsible for the injury that comes to the world through the decline of the ministry and the neglect of God and His word. Such is your responsibility if you let the ministry decline; and if you do

---

*Deut. v. 9.

not feel enough interest to give your child, you would act the same if all the children in the world were yours,—so that as far as you are concerned the service of God would perish.

And it does no good to say: "My neighbor keeps his son at school, I dare not do it," and so forth. For your neighbor can say the same thing, and so on with all neighbors; and where then will God find people for the ministerial office? You have children, and can give them, but will not do it; thus, so far as you are concerned, the ministry falls to the ground. And because you with gross ingratitude let the sacred office, so dearly purchased, languish and die, you will be accursed, and in your own person, or in your children, you will suffer shame and sorrow, or otherwise be so tormented, that you will be damned with them, not only here on earth, but eternally in hell. This will not fail to come upon you, in order that you may learn that your children are not so entirely your own, that you can withhold them from God; He will have justice, and they are more His than yours.

PART FIRST.

The Spiritual Benefit or Injury arising from the Support or Neglect of Schools.

And that you may not think that I speak too harshly,

I will lay before you in part (for who can tell all?) the benefit or the injury that you are doing, so that, in case you find yourself guilty, and do not amend your ways, you will be obliged to say yourselves, that you verily belong to the devil, and deserve to be condemned to hell; or so that, on the other hand, you may heartily rejoice and be glad if you find yourself chosen of God, to educate with your means and labor a son, who will become a pious Christian pastor, preacher, or schoolmaster, and thus to bring up for God an especial servant—yea, as was said above, a messenger of God, a pious bishop, a saviour of many people, a king and prince in the kingdom of Christ, a teacher among God's people, a light of the world. And who will or can relate all the honor and excellence that a good and faithful pastor has before God? There is no more precious treasure, no nobler thing on earth, than a pious, faithful pastor or preacher.

For consider that whatever of good is connected with the office of preaching and the care of souls, will be accomplished by your son, if he is faithful in his ministry, so that through him many souls will be daily taught, converted, baptized, brought to Christ, made blessed, redeemed from sin, death, hell, and the devil, and come to perfect righteousness and eternal life in heaven. Daniel well says: "They that teach others shall shine as the brightness of the firmament; and they that turn many to righteousness, as the stars forever and ever" (Dan. xii. 3). For since God's Word and office, where they are rightly employed, must always accomplish great things, and indeed work miracles, your son will be constantly doing wonderful things for God, such as to raise the dead, cast out devils, make the blind to see, the deaf to hear, the lepers to be clean, the dumb to speak, and the lame to walk. If this is not done in the body, it is done in the soul, which is indeed a greater work, as Christ says, John xiv. 12: "He that believeth on me, the works that I do shall he do also; and greater works than these shall he do." If a simple Christian can do such things in the case of individuals, how much more can a public preacher accomplish, who deals with whole congregations? Not that he does it himself, but his office, which has been instituted of God for that purpose, and the Word of God, which he teaches; for he is but an instrument in the hands of God.

If he does such great works and miracles spiritually, it follows that he does them also physically, or at least is a beginner and cause of them. For whence comes it that Christians will rise from the dead on the day of judgment?—that all the deaf, blind, lame, and all other sufferers will throw off their bodily ailments, and that their bodies will not simply become beautiful and sound, but, as Christ says, shine bright and glorious as the sun? Does it not come from the fact that here on earth, through the Word of God, they have been converted, baptized, and united to Christ? As Paul says, Rom. viii. 11: "He that raised up Christ from the dead shall also quicken your mortal bodies by His Spirit that dwelleth in you." Who helps men to such faith, and the beginning of the bodily resurrection, without the office of preaching and the Word of God, which are committed to your son? Is that not an immeasurably grander and more splendid work and miracle, than if He raised the dead here in the world, and restored the blind, deaf, dumb, and leprous to a perishable existence?

If you were certain that your son would perform one of these works on a single individual, so that he would make a blind man to see, raise a man from the dead, rescue a soul from the devil, or save a human being from hell, would you not properly, with all joy, use your means to educate him for such an office and work? And would you not leap for joy that with your money you had accomplished so great a thing for God? For what are all endowments and cloisters, as they now exist with their own works, in comparison with such a pastor, preacher, or school-master?

although in former times they were established by pious kings and lords for this precious end, that they might be agencies for bringing up such pastors and preachers; but now alas! through the influence of the devil, they have sunk into degradation, so that they have become, to the injury and destruction of Christianity, the suburbs of hell.

Behold, thy son performs not only one such work, but many, and that every day; and what is best of all, he does them in the sight of God, who holds them dear, as has been shown, though men do not recognize and esteem them; yea, if the world regard him as a heretic, seducer, deceiver, so much the better: it is a good sign that he is an upright man, and like the Lord Jesus Christ. For Christ himself was held a deceiver, rebel, and criminal, and was judged and crucified with murderers. Were I a preacher, what would it concern me that the world called me a devil, if I knew that God called me an angel? Let the world call me a seducer as long as it pleases—if God but call me his faithful servant and steward, the angels call me their companion, the saints call me their brother, the believing call me their father, distressed souls call me their saviour, the ignorant call me their light, and God approves of it all, what harm can the world and the devil do me with their calumny and abuse?

We have been speaking of the works and miracles which your son does in relation to souls, in saving them from sin, death, and the devil. But in relation to the world also he does great and mighty works, in that he informs and instructs all classes how they are to discharge their various duties in a manner acceptable to God. He comforts the sorrowing, gives counsel, settles difficulties, calms disturbed consciences, helps to maintain peace, to appease, to reconcile, and similar duties without number; for a preacher confirms, strengthens, and supports all authority, all temporal peace, governs the seditious, teaches obedience, morality, discipline, and honor, and gives instruction in the duties pertaining to fathers, mothers, children, servants, and in a word to all other secular relations of life. These are, it is true, the least of a pastor's services; yet they are so excellent and noble that the wisest of the heathen philosophers did not recognize or understand, much less practice them; and no jurist, no university, no cloister, knows of such works, nor are they taught in either ecclesiastical or civil law. For there is no one who recognizes such secular offices as the great gifts or gracious arrangement of God; it is the Word of God and the ministerial office alone that highly praise and honor them.

Therefore, if we wish to speak the truth, we must

say that temporal peace—the greatest good on earth, in which all other temporal blessings are comprehended—is really a fruit of the ministerial office. For where it perishes, there are found war, hatred, and the shedding of blood; and where it is not properly exercised, we find, if not actual war, at least a constant unrest, a desire for war and bloodshed. We see this exemplified in the case of the Papists, who can do nothing but shout fire and blood, and who murder innocent pastors on account of marriage, though the Pope himself and their own ecclesiastical law only sanction as the highest punishment for such an offense expulsion from the priestly office, according the offenders life, and property, and Christian integrity; and so far from condemning them to hell, they do not even hold them as heretics, as all the jurists and the world at large must testify, and as the imperial Diet at Nuremberg decreed. But the blind bloodhounds who have turned the clerical office into a lie, can not desist from murder, as their god the devil also does, who from the beginning has been a murderer and liar. (John viii. 44.)

An upright pastor, then, serves mankind in body and soul, in estate and honor. But above that, consider how he serves God, and what splendid sacrifices and services he renders: for through his office and

Word, the kingdom of God is maintained in the world, the honor, the name, the glory of God, a right faith and apprehension of Christ, the fruit of the suffering, and blood, and death of Christ, the gifts, works and power of the Holy Spirit, the proper use of Baptism and the Lord's Supper, the pure doctrine of the Gospel, the proper manner of chastening and crucifying the flesh, and similar blessings. Who can sufficiently extol a single one of them? And how much remains to be said! The faithful pastor fights against the devil, worldly wisdom, spiritual blindness; he gains victories over them, strikes down error, suppresses heresies. For he must strive and battle against the gates of hell, overcome the devil, which he also does, not by his own might, but through his office and word. These are all inexpressible works and miracles of the ministerial office. In a word, if we praise God himself, we must also praise the Word and preaching; for it is the office and Word of God.

If you were a king, you should yet esteem yourself unworthy to consecrate your son, with all your property, to such an office and work. Is not the labor or the penny that you bestow on such a son, too highly honored, too richly blessed, too costly invested, and in the eyes of God is it not better than any kingdom or empire? A man ought to carry such a penny to the ends of the earth, if he knew that it would be so splendidly invested. And behold, you have in your own house and in your own bosom the means of this priceless investment. Shame, and again I say shame upon our blind and base ingratitude, that we do not see what a beautiful and excellent service we render to God, yea, what great personages we may become in His sight, with little effort and expense.

The Papists abuse us Lutherans for not teaching good works. They are fine fellows to talk about good works! Are not the things just mentioned good works? What are all the works of the priests and monks in comparison with such miracles? Their talk is like the chattering of jackdaws, only not so good; for the jackdaws chatter from love and pleasure, but the Papists howl from chagrin. If people have heretofore set great store by the first mass and a new priest; if father and mother with their friends have rejoiced because they had brought up a son to be an idle, lazy, useless priest of the mass or of the cupboard, who with his blasphemous sacrifice of the mass and his reprobate prayers insults God, and vexes and flays society: how much more should you rejoice, if you bring up a son for one of these callings, in which you are sure that he grandly serves God, richly aids mankind, and heroically fights the devil? Here you make a true sacrifice of your son, so that the angels are obliged to regard you with admiration.

Again, you should also know the injury you do, if you take the opposite course. For if God has given you a child suitable for such an office, and you do not bring him up for it, thinking only of his temporal wants; take up the list of good works and miracles above given, and examine it, and you will find what a hypocrite you are. For as far as lies in your power, you deprive God of a messenger, a servant, a king and prince in his kingdom, a saviour and comforter of man in body and soul, in estate and honor, a captain and knight to contend against the devil; and at the same time you make room for the devil, and advance his kingdom, by helping him to keep souls in sin, death, hell, and daily to bring many more under his power; you aid in perpetuating heresy, error, discontent, war, and hate in the world, whereby it daily becomes worse; and thus the kingdom of God, Christian faith, the fruit of the suffering and blood of Christ, the work of the Holy Spirit, the Gospel and all worship of God perish, while the service of Satan and fatal errors gain the ascendency. This condition of things would have been hindered and bettered, if you had brought up your child to the ministry.

How will it be with you, when God on your death-bed, or in the day of judgment, thus addresses you: " I was hungry, thirsty, a guest, naked, sick, in prison, and you did not help me; for what you have not done to my people and kindom and Gospel on earth, helping to destroy them and allowing souls to perish, you have not done to me. For you could have helped me; I had given you children and property; but you stubbornly permitted me and my kingdom and the souls of men to suffer want and to be despised, while in opposition to me you served Satan and his kingdom. He shall now be your reward; depart with him into the abyss of hell! You have not helped to build up and advance my kingdom, but to weaken and destroy it; you have helped to promote the interests and power of the devil: dwell then in the house you have built."

What do you think? Are you not in danger that the wrath of God may suddenly overtake you, who go on heedlessly, as if you were doing right in not instructing your children? And when his judgment comes, you will have to say that you are righteously condemned to hell as one of the most impious and most hurtful of men. And if you would now, in the present life, rightly consider the matter, you would be filled with terror; for no conscience is able to bear the guilt of a single one of the particulars mentioned above;

how much less can it bear the burden of all when they suddenly fall upon the soul? Your heart will then cry out that your sins are more numerous than the leaves of the forest, greater than heaven and earth, and with Manasseh, king of Judah, you will exclaim: "My sins are more than the sands of the seashore, and my offense is great."

Our natural sense of right attests this truth, that whoever can prevent an injury, and does not do it, he is guilty of the injury, since he evidently has a desire and will for it, and would do it himself, if he had cause and opportunity. Therefore such people are no better than Satan himself, because they are so hostile to God and the world, that they help to overthrow religion and social order, and faithfully serve the devil. In a word, if we can denounce Satan enough, we can denounce such people enough, who hinder the office and work ordained of God: for they are the servants of the devil.

I do not mean that every one is obliged to bring up his child to such an office, for all boys are not to become pastors, preachers, school-masters; and it is well to know that the children of lords and nobles are not to be thus employed, since society needs them for secular authority and social order. I speak of the common people, who would formerly have schooled their children for the sake of a benefice and an income, and who now only on account of support withhold them from the office, although they need no heirs, and keep their children from school, notwithstanding the fact that their children are well adapted to the ministry, and could serve God without want or hindrance.

Such promising children should be instructed, especially the children of the poor; for this purpose the revenues of endowments and monasteries were provided. But also the boys that are less promising should learn at least to understand, read, and write Latin. For we need not only learned doctors and masters in the Scriptures, but also ordinary pastors, who may teach the Gospel and the catechism to the young and ignorant, baptize, administer the Lord's Supper, &c. If they are not capable of contending with heretics, it does not matter. For in a good building, we need both large and small timber; and in like manner we must have sextons and others to aid the minister and further the Word of God.

And if such a boy who has learned Latin afterwards works at a trade, you will have him in reserve, to labor as a pastor in case of need; and such knowledge will not interfere with his gaining a livelihood, and will enable him to govern his house all the better. And especially in our times is it easy to educate such persons, who may learn the Gospel and the catechism, because not only the Holy Scriptures but also every kind of learning is now within reach, with so many books and so much reading and preaching that (God be thanked!) a man at present can learn more in three years than formerly in twenty; even women and children can now learn more of God and Christ from German books and sermons (I speak the truth) than was formerly known by the universities, priests, monks, the whole Papacy, and the entire world. But even the ordinary pastor and preacher must be acquainted with Latin, which he can no more dispense with than the learned can dispense with Greek and Hebrew, as St. Augustine says, and ecclesiastical law itself establishes.

But you say, "How if it turns out badly, so that my son becomes a heretic or a villain?" For, as people say, "education means perversion." Well, you must run that risk; but your labor is not lost. God will consider your faithful service, and will count it as if successful. You must run the risk, as in other callings to which you wish to bring up your son. How was it with Abraham, whose son Ishmael did badly; with Isaac and his son Esau; with Adam and his son Cain? Ought Abraham for that reason to have neglected his son Isaac, Isaac his son Jacob, and Adam his son

Abel? Among the chosen children of Israel, how many wicked kings and people there were, who with their heresy and idolatry wrought all manner of evil and slew the prophets: would it therefore have been right for the priests to neglect the whole people, and educate no one for the service of God? How many wicked priests and Levites were in the tribe of Levi, which God himself chose for the priestly office? How many people has God on earth who abuse all his goodness? Should He therefore withhold His goodness, suffer all men to perish, and cease to do well?

You should not be anxious in regard to the support of your son in case he devotes himself to learning and the ministry, for God has not forsaken and forgotten you in this particular. He has ordained through St. Paul, 1 Cor. ix. 14, "that they which preach the Gospel should live of the Gospel." And Christ himself has said, Matt. x. 10, that "the workman is worthy of his meat." In the Old Testament, in order that the ministerial office might not perish, God chose and took the whole tribe of Levi, that is to say, the twelfth part of the whole people of Israel, and gave them "the tenth in Israel for an inheritance," and in addition the first fruits, all kinds of offerings, their own cities, land, and cattle, and whatever belongs thereto. In the New Testament era, see how richly in former times emperors, kings, princes and lords, contributed to the support of this office, so that churches and monasteries now surpass kings and princes in wealth. God will not and can not forsake his faithful servants, as He has promised, Heb. xiii. 5: "I will never leave thee nor forsake thee."

Consider for yourselves how many pastorates, schools, and other offices are daily becoming vacant. That fact assures your son of a support before he needs it or has earned it. When I was a young student, I heard it said that in Saxony, if I mistake not, there were about eighteen hundred parishes. If that is true, and if with each parish two persons, a pastor and a sexton, are connected (not counting the preachers, chaplains, assistants, and teachers in the cities), it follows that about four thousand learned persons belong to such a principality, of whom one-third die in ten years. Now I would wager that there are not four thousand students in the half of Germany. I venture the assertion also that there are scarcely eight hundred pastors in Saxony;—how many must be wanting in all Germany?

I should like to know where in three years we are to get pastors, teachers, and sextons? If we remain idle, and if the princes in particular do not see to it that both preparatory schools and universities are properly maintained, there will be such a want of educated persons, that three or four cities will have to be assigned to one pastor, and ten villages to one chaplain, if perchance the ministers can be found at all.

It is sad to see how the universities of Erfurt, Leipsic, and others, as well as the preparatory schools, are deserted, so that little Wittenberg almost alone is doing its best. This same want, I imagine, will be felt also by the chapters and monasteries, who will not continue to boast as they have begun. Hence you can send your son to school with full assurance that men will be wanting rather than means; and perchance, if the world lasts and God graciously influences princes and cities to act, the property of chapters and cloisters may be applied to this purpose, for which it was originally designed. And why care so much for the body? There stands Christ and says, Matt. vi. 31, 33: "Take no thought, saying, what shall we eat? or, what shall we drink? or, wherewithal shall we be clothed? For your heavenly Father knoweth that ye have need of all these things. But seek ye first the kingdom of God and his righteousness, and all these things shall be added unto you." Whoever does not believe that, let him take anxious thought, and yet die of hunger.

Though it is true that some years ago many pastors suffered hunger and destitution, the reason is to be found in the great commotion prevailing in the world, so that people became wicked, ungrateful, and avaricious, and persecuted the Gospel. It was thus that God tried us, in order to see if we were sincere; and we are not to regard this trial otherwise than in the days of the martyrs, when pious teachers suffered great poverty and want, as St. Paul himself boasts. And Christ also predicted, Matt. ix. 15: "When the bridegroom shall be taken from them, then shall they fast." That is true, evangelical fasting.

God's Word has seldom appeared without being attended with scarcity or famine, as in the days of Abraham, Isaac, Jacob, Joseph, Elijah, Elisha; and in the early days of the Gospel, there was a "great dearth throughout all the world." (Acts xi. 28). And the blame is ascribed to the precious Gospel and the Word of God, and not to the past sins and present obdurate ingratitude of men. Thus the Jews attributed all their misfortune to the teaching of Jeremiah (Jer. xliv. 16-19). And the Romans, when they were overthrown by the Goths, ascribed their defeat to the fact that they had become Christians, against which error St. Augustine wrote a great book, "De Civitate Dei."

But say what we will, the world is the world: as those became deceivers and perished, so shall also these become deceivers and perish, that Christ and His word may remain. He sits exalted and immovable, as it is written: "The Lord said unto my Lord, sit thou on my right hand." He can not be moved; and so long as He remains, we shall remain also. And in a word, it would be as easy for your son to secure a support from the ministry as from a trade, if property is what you are after, in order to make a great lord of your son in the eyes of the world, like the bishops and canons. But if you are thus minded, this discourse is not addressed to you.

I speak to the believing, who honor the ministerial office, and esteem it far above wealth as, next to God himself, the best treasure given to men, in order that they may know what a great service they render God, when they prefer this work with little pay to the world's riches without it. They will not fail to recognize that the soul is more than the body, and that the body may be easily provided for, all superfluities being left behind at death. But those who seek true riches will take their treasure with them, which is far better. So much for a brief and hasty consideration of the benefit and the injury resulting from a maintenance or a neglect of the schools.

PART SECOND.

The Temporal Benefit or Injury arising from the Support or the Neglect of Schools.

The second part of this discourse will be devoted to the temporal or secular benefit and injury resulting from a support or a neglect of schools. In the first place, it is true that secular authority or station is in no way comparable to the spiritual office of the ministry, as St. Paul calls it; for it is not so dearly purchased through the blood and death of the Son of God. It can not perform such great works and miracles as the ministerial office; for all the works of secular authority belong only to this temporal and transitory existence, such as caring for body, wife, child, house, goods, and honor, and whatever else pertains to the needs of the present life. As far then as eternal life surpasses temporal life, so far does the ministerial office surpass secular office; the one is the substance, the other is the shadow. For secular authority is an image, shadow, or figure of the authority of Christ; for the ministerial office, (where it exists as God ordained it,) brings and imparts eternal righteousness, eternal peace, and eternal life, as St. Paul declares in the fourth chapter of 2 Corinthians. But secular government maintains temporal and transitory peace, law, and life.

But it is still a beautiful and divine ordinance, an excellent gift of God, who ordained it, and who wishes to have it maintained as indispensable to human welfare; without it men could not live together in society, but would devour one another like the irrational animals. Therefore, as it is the function and honor of the ministerial office to make saints out of sinners, to restore the dead to life, to confer blessedness upon the lost, to change the servants of the devil into children of God: so it is the function and honor of civil government to make men out of wild animals, and to restrain them from degenerating into brutes. It protects every one in body, so that he may not be injured; it protects every one in family, so that the members may not be wronged; it protects every one in house, lands, cattle, property, so that they may not be attacked, injured, or stolen.

This state of things does not exist among the lower animals, and it would not prevail among men, if it were not for civil government. If the birds and beasts could speak, and should consider the civil regulations of men, do you not suppose that they would say: "O ye men, in comparison with us ye are gods! In what security ye live and possess all things! But we are not secure against one another for an hour in life, home or food. Woe to your ingratitude, that ye do not perceive what an excellent gift the God of us all has bestowed upon you!"

Since then it is certain that civil government is a divine ordinance, an office and institution necessary for men in the present life, it is easy to see that God does not design that it should perish, but that it should continue for the protection of the righteous and the punishment of the wicked, as is clearly taught in Romans xiii. 4 and 1 Peter ii. 13. But who will maintain it except us men to whom God has committed it? Wild animals will not do it, wood and stone will not; but what men can maintain it? Certainly not those who rule by club-law alone, as many now think. For where club-law alone prevails, will surely be found at last a brutal condition of society, the strong tyrannizing over the weak. We have examples enough before our eyes to show us what sheer physical force, without wisdom or reason, would do.

Hence Solomon says in Proverbs viii. 14, 15, that wisdom must rule, and not force, testifying of the former: "Counsel is mine and sound wisdom; I am understanding; I have strength. By me kings reign, and princes decree justice." And in Ecclesiastes ix. 16, 18, he says: "Wisdom is better than strength. Wisdom is better than weapons of war." All history shows that mere force, without reason or wisdom, can never accomplish anything; and even tyrants and murderers, unless they wisely cloak their tyranny under the forms of law and right, can not long continue in authority, but soon disagree and perish by one another's hand. In a word, not club-law but justice, not force but wisdom and reason, must govern among the wicked as well as among the good.

Accordingly, since our government in the German states is based on the imperial law of Rome, which embodies the wisdom and reason of our government, it follows that such a government can not be maintained, unless these laws are upheld. Now who will uphold them? Club-law and force will not do it; it must be done by means of knowledge and books; men must learn and understand the law and wisdom of our empire. Although it is an excellent thing when an emperor, prince or lord is wise and judicious by nature, so that he can administer justice without external aids, as could Frederick, Duke of Saxony, and Fabian von Feilitz (not to speak of the living); yet such rulers are rare, and their example is dangerous, so that it is always better to adhere to the written law, which carries with it authority, and serves as a safeguard against arbitrary action.

Now in civil government it is the jurists and scholars who uphold this law, and thereby maintain secular authority; and just as a pious theologian or sincere preacher in the kingdom of Christ is called a messenger of God, a saviour, prophet, priest, steward and teacher (as was said above), in like manner a pious jurist or a faithful scholar in the government of the emperor might be called a prophet, priest, messenger, and saviour. On the other hand, just as a heretic or hypocritical minister in the kingdom of Christ is a devil, thief, murderer, blasphemer; in the same way a corrupt and unfaithful jurist in the government of the emperor is a thief, rogue, traitor, devil.

When I speak of jurists, I do not mean the doctors alone, but the whole body of civil officers—chancellors, secretaries, judges, advocates, notaries, and whatever else belongs to the civil administration, even the great crowd of advisers, as they are called, at court; for they exercise the functions of law and of jurists. And since an adviser through evil advice can easily become a traitor, it sometimes happens that under the form of friendly counsel sovereigns are basely betrayed.

You now see of what use an upright jurist can be; yea, who can fully set it forth? For whatever is God's ordinance and work, bears so much fruit that it can not be told or comprehended. First of all, such a jurist maintains and furthers with his legal knowledge (through divine institution) the whole structure of civil government—emperors, princes, lords, cities, states, people (as before stated), for all must be upheld through wisdom and justice. But who can sufficiently praise this work alone? It gives you protection of body and life against neighbors, enemies, murderers; protection also of wife, daughters, sons, house, servants, money, property, lands, and whatever you possess; for it is all comprehended, secured, and hedged about by law. How great a blessing that is, can not be told. Who can express the immeasurable benefits of peace? How much it gives and saves every year!

Such great works can your son do, and such a useful person can he become, if you direct him to the civil service and send him to school; and if you can become a sharer in this honor, and make such good use of your money, ought it not to be a great pleasure and glory to you? Think of your son as a messenger in the empire, an apostle of the emperor, a cornerstone and foundation of temporal peace on earth! Knowing, too, that God looks upon the service in this light, as indeed it deserves to be! For though we can not be justified and secure salvation by such works, it is still a joyful comfort that these works are well-pleasing to God, especially when such a man is a believer and a member of Christ's kingdom; for in that way we thank him for his benefits, and bring him the best thank-offering and the highest service.

You must indeed be an insensible and ungrateful creature, fit to be ranked among the brutes, if you see that your son may become a man to help the emperor maintain his dominions, sword, and crown—to help the prince govern his land, to counsel cities and states, to help protect for every man his body, wife, child, property, and honor—and yet will not do so much as to send him to school and prepare him for this work! Tell me, what are all the chapters and cloisters doing in comparison with this? I would not give the work of a faithful, upright jurist and secretary for the righteousness of all the monks, priests, and nuns at their best. And if such great good works do not move you, the honor and desire of God alone should move you, since you know that you thereby express your gratitude to God, and render Him a service of surpassing excellence, as has been said. It is a shameful contempt of God that you do not bring up your children to such an excellent and divinely appointed calling, and that you strengthen them only in the service of appetite and avarice, teaching them nothing but to provide for the stomach, like a hog with its nose always in filth, and do not bring them up to this worthy station and office. You must either be insensible creatures, or else you do not love your children.

But hearken further: how if God demands your child for such office? For you are under obligation to help maintain civil order if you can. Now, beyond all doubt, it can not be maintained if people do not have their children instructed; and since more wisdom is required in civil office than in the ministry, it will be necessary to set apart for it the brightest boys. For in the ministry Christ works by His Spirit; but in civil government men must be guided by reason (which is the source of human laws): for God has placed secular government and our physical state under the control of reason (Gen. ii. 19), and has not sent the Holy Spirit for that purpose. Hence the functions of civil office are more difficult than those of the ministry, since the conscience can not rule, but must act, so to speak, in the dark.

If now you have a son capable of learning; if you can send him to school, but do not do it and go your way asking nothing about temporal government, law, peace, and so on; you are, to the extent of your ability, opposing civil authority like the Turk, yea, like the devil himself. For you withhold from the empire, principality, state, city, a saviour, comforter, corner-stone, helper; and so far as you are concerned, the emperor loses both his sword and crown, the state loses protection and peace, and it is through your fault (as much as lies in you) that no man can hold in security his body, wife, child, house, property. On the contrary, you freely offer them all upon a butcher's block, and give occasion for men to degenerate into brutes, and at last to devour one another. All this you certainly do, especially if you on purpose withdraw your child from such a salutary station out of regard for his physical wants. Are you not a pretty and useful man in society! You daily enjoy the benefits of the government, and then as a return rob it of your son, dedicating him to avarice, and thus strive with all your might not to maintain government, law, and peace, but to destroy social order, though you possess and hold your body, life, property, and honor, through secular authority.

What do you think you deserve? Are you even worthy to dwell among men? What will God say, who has given you child and property that you might honor Him therewith, and consecrate your child to His service? Is it not serving God, if we help to maintain His ordinance of civil government? Now you neglect such service, as if it did not concern you, or as if you above all men were free and not bound to serve God; and you presume to do with your child what you please, even though the temporal and the spiritual kingdom of God perish; and at the same time you enjoy the protection, peace, and law of the empire, and allow the ministry and Word of God to serve you, so that God becomes your servant: and yet you abuse all these benefits to turn your son from him, and to teach him the service of Mammon.

Do you not think God will pronounce such a judgment on your worldliness that you will perish with your children and property? Rather, is not your heart affrighted at the horror of your idolatry, at your contempt of God, your ingratitude, your destruction of the civil and religious ordinances of God, yea, at the injury you do all men? Well, I have declared unto you both the benefit and the injury you can do; and do which you will, God will surely repay you.

I will not here speak of the pleasure a scholar has, apart from any office, in that he can read at home all kinds of books, talk and associate with learned men, and travel and transact business in foreign lands. For this pleasure perhaps will move but few; but since you are seeking Mammon and worldly possessions, consider what great opportunities God has provided for schools and scholars; so that you need not despise learning from fear of poverty. Behold, emperors and kings must have chancellors, secretaries, counsellors, jurists and scholars; there is not a prince but must have chancellors, jurists, counsellors, scholars, and secretaries; likewise counts, lords, cities, states, castles, must have councils, secretaries, and other learned men; there is not a nobleman but must have a secretary. And to speak of ordinary scholars, where are the miners, merchants, and artisans? At the end of three years where are we to find educated men, when the want has already begun to be felt? It looks as if kings would have to become jurists, princes chancellors, counts and lords secretaries, and mayors sextons.

If we do not soon begin to do something, we shall become Tartars and Turks, and ignoramuses will again be doctors and counsellors at court. Therefore I hold that there never was a better time for study than the present, not only because learning is so accessible and cheap, but also because great wealth and honor must follow; for those who study at this time will become such valuable people that two princes and three cities will contend for one scholar. If you look about you, you will find innumerable offices that will need learned men in less than ten years, and yet but few young people are being educated for them.

There is further a divine blessing attached to this sphere of activity; for God is pleased with the many excellent and useful works that belong to the secular condition, and that constitute a divine service. But avarice in seeking its end meets with contempt (even though its works be not sinful); evil deeds destroy all peace of mind, and such a life can not be called a service of God. Now I would rather earn ten florins with a work that might properly be called a service of God, than a thousand florins with a work that could not be called a service of God, but a service of self and Mammon.

In addition to this, there is worldly honor. For chancellors, scribes, jurists, and the people through them, occupy upper seats, help, advise and govern as said above, and in fact they here become lords on earth, though in person, birth, and station they are not so regarded. For Daniel says that he did the king's work. And it is true that a chancellor must perform imperial, kingly, princely functions and duties, a city scribe must do the work of the council and city, and that all with honor and the blessing of God, which gives happiness and salvation.

When they are not engaged in war but govern by law, what are emperors, kings, princes, (if we speak according to their work,) but mere scribes and jurists? For they concern themselves about the law, which is a legal and clerical work. And who governs the land and people in times of peace? Is it the knights and captains? I think it is the pen of the scribe. Meanwhile, what is avarice doing with its worship of Mammon? It can not come to such honor, and defiles its devotees with its rust-covered treasures.

Thus the emperor Justinian declares that "imperial majesty ought not only to be adorned with arms, but also to be armed with laws." Observe the peculiar phraseology this emperor uses, when he calls the laws his weapons, and weapons his adornment, and changes his scribes into cuirassiers and warriors. And he spoke well; for the laws are truly the right armor and weapons with which to protect the country and people, yea, the empire and government, (as has been sufficiently shown above,) so that wisdom is better than might. And pious jurists are the real warriors that preserve the emperor and princes. How many passages, if time permitted, might be given from the poets and the historians! Solomon himself in Ecclesisastes ix. 15 declares that a poor man by his wisdom saved a city from a powerful king.

Not that I would have soldiers, knights, and whatever else belongs to warfare, despised and repudiated; they also help (where they are obedient) to maintain peace and protect the land by force. Every thing has its honor before God, and its station and work.

I must also praise my craft, though I should be cen-

DUTY OF SENDING CHILDREN TO SCHOOL.

sured; just as St. Paul constantly praised his office, so that many thought he went too far and was proud. Whoever wishes to praise and honor soldiers, can find ground enough to do so, as I have elsewhere shown in strong terms. For I do not like those jurists and scribblers who have so high an opinion of themselves that they despise or mock other callings, as the extortionate priests and other adherents of the Papacy have hitherto done.

We should duly praise all the offices and works ordained of God, and not despise one for the sake of another; for it is written, "His work is honorable and glorious" (Ps. iii. 3). And again, Psalm civ. 24: "O Lord, how manifold are thy works! in wisdom hast thou made them all." And especially should preachers constantly inculcate such thoughts upon the people, school-teachers likewise upon their pupils, and parents upon their children, that these may learn what stations and offices are ordained of God. When they come to understand this, they should not despise, mock, or speak evil of them, but honor and esteem them. That is pleasing to God, and contributes to peace and unity; for God is a great Lord, and has many servants.

On the contrary, we find some conceited soldiers that fancy the name scribe is not worthy to be mentioned or heard by them. Well, pay no attention to it, but consider that these poor fellows must have some kind of pastime and pleasure. Let them make the most out of this; but you still remain a scribe in the eyes of God and the world. If they come together for any length of time, you see that they bestow the highest honor upon the quill, placing a feather on hat or helmet, as if they confessed by that act that the pen is the most excellent thing in the world, without which they would not be equipped for combat, nor for parade in times of peace, much less assemble in security; for they must also profit by the peace which the emperor's preachers and teachers (the jurists) maintain. Therefore, as you see, they give the place of honor to the instrument of our craft (and properly), since they gird the sword about the loins; there it hangs handsomely for their purpose: on the head it would not be becoming—there the feather must wave. If they have sinned against you, they have thus made atonement and should be forgiven.

The work of the scholar, as I have shown, is not appreciated by many ignoramuses; for they do not know that it is a divine office and function, nor consider how necessary and useful it is to the world. But let them go, and look about you for wise and pious noblemen, as Duke George of Werdheim, Hans

DUTY OF SENDING CHILDREN TO SCHOOL. 257

von Schwartzenberg, George von Fronsberg, and others of blessed memory, (I shall not speak of the living,) and comfort yourself in them. Consider that God, for the sake of one man, Lot, honored the whole city of Zoar; for the sake of Naaman, the whole land of Syria; and for the sake of Joseph, the whole kingdom of Egypt; and why should not you, for the sake of many worthy men, honor all the nobility? Think rather of the good than of the bad. Do not condemn the tree, because perchance some of its fruit falls untimely or becomes a prey to worms.

Thus do the children of God. For God spares the whole human race for the sake of one man, who is called Jesus Christ. If he were to look on mankind alone, there could be nothing but anger. Yet the ministry and the civil authorities are necessarily required to pay attention to evil, for they should punish the wicked; some by reproof, and some by the sword. But we should learn to distinguish between what is God's work and what is man's wickedness. In all divine offices and stations there are many wicked men; but the office still remains good, however much men may abuse it. We find, for example, many bad women, dishonest servants, and injurious officers and counsellors; and yet all these relations and conditions are the work and ordinance of God. The sun remains good, though the whole world abuse its light, some to rob, some to murder, and some to work other evils. Who could do evil if the sun did not give light, if the earth did not bring forth fruit, if the air did not remain pure, and if God did not thus exercise a constant care? It is written, "The creature was made subject to vanity, not willingly," Rom. viii. 20.

There are some who think that the office of scribe is an easy, insignificant office, but that to ride in armor and suffer heat, frost, dust, thirst, and other discomforts, is work. Verily that is an old story—no one knows where the shoe pinches another; every one feels only his own discomfort, and looks only at the comforts of another. It is true that it would be hard for me to ride in armor; but I should like to see the knight who could sit still the whole day and look in a book, though he were not required to read, think, or do any thing. Ask a chancery-clerk, preacher, orator, about the labor of writing and speaking; ask a school-master about the labor of teaching boys. The pen is a light instrument, it is true, and among all the trades there is no tool more easily procured than the pen; for it needs only a goose-quill, which can be found anywhere. But the best part of the body, as the head, and the noblest member, as the tongue, and the highest function, as speech, must here bear the brunt, and do most of the work, while in other occupations it is the hands, feet, back that labor, and the workman can at the same time sing and joke, which a writer must forego. Three fingers do it, (as is said of writers,) but the whole body and soul work at the same time.

When the ignoramuses about the illustrious emperor Maximilian complained that he employed so many scribes for embassies and other similar duties, he is said to have replied: "What shall I do? You cannot be employed, so I must take scribes." And further: "I can make knights, but not doctors." I have heard also of a wise nobleman who said: "I shall let my son study; there is no great art in straddling a horse and becoming a knight,—a thing that is soon learned." And that is all well said.

I do not say this to depreciate the knightly order or any other, but to rebuke the ignorant fellows who despise all learning and culture, and praise nothing but wearing armor and straddling a horse, though they are seldom obliged to do it, and hence, the whole year through, have comfort, pleasure, honor, and money. It is indeed true that learning is light to carry, and that armor is heavy to carry; but on the other hand, to wear armor is easily learned, but an education is neither quickly acquired nor easily employed.

But to make an end of this matter, God is a wonderful sovereign, and it is his plan of work to make lords out of beggars, as he made the heaven and earth out of nothing; and in this no man will hinder Him, who is praised in all the world, as the 112th Psalm says: "Who is like unto the Lord our God, who dwelleth on high, who humbleth Himself to behold the things that are in heaven and in the earth? He raiseth up the poor out of the dust, and lifteth the needy out of the dunghill; that He may set him with princes, even with the princes of His people." Look at all the courts of kings and princes, and in cities and pastorates, and do you not see this Psalm fulfilled by many striking examples? You will there find jurists, doctors, counselors, scribes, preachers, who struggled with poverty in acquiring an education, and who have risen by means of the pen to the position of lords, as this Psalm says, and like princes they help to govern the land and people. God does not wish that those who are born kings, princes, lords, and nobles should alone rule, but He desires also to have His beggars share in the government; otherwise, they would think that noble birth alone made lords and rulers, and that God had nothing to do with it.

It is true, as is sometimes said, that the Pope was once a student; therefore do not despise the boys who beg from door to door "a little bread for the love of God,"* and when the groups of poor pupils sing before your house, remember that you hear, as this Psalm says, great princes and lords. I have myself been such a beggar pupil, and have eaten bread before houses, especially in the dear town of Eisenach, though afterwards my beloved father supported me at the University of Erfurt with all love and self-sacrifice, and by the sweat of his face helped me to the position I now occupy; but still I was for a time a poverty student, and according to this Psalm I have risen by the pen to a position which I would not exchange for that of the Turkish sultan, taking his wealth and giving up my learning. Yea, I would not exchange it for all the wealth of the world many times multiplied; and yet, beyond all doubt, I should not have attained my present station, if I had not gone to school and learned to write.

Without anxiety, then, let your son study, and if he should have to beg bread for a time, you give our God material out of which he can make a lord. It will remain true that your son and mine, that is to say, the children of the common people, will rule the world, both in spiritual and secular stations, as this Psalm testifies. For wealthy worldlings can not and

---

*Panem propter Deum.

will not do it; they are the priests and monks of Mammon, upon whom they are obliged to wait day and night; princes and lords by birth can not do it alone, and especially are they unable to fill the spiritual office of the ministry. Thus must both spiritual and secular government continue on earth in the hands of the common people and their children.

And pay no attention to the contempt which the ordinary devotee of Mammon manifests for culture, so that he says: "Well, if my son can read, write, and cipher, that is enough; for I am going to make a merchant out of him?" Without scholars it would not be long till business men in their perplexity would be ready to dig a learned man out of the ground ten yards deep with their fingers; for the merchant will not long remain a merchant, if preaching and the administration of justice cease. I know full well that we theologians and jurists must remain, or else all other vocations will inevitably go to the ground with us; where theologians perish, there perishes also the Word of God, and nothing but heathen and devils are left; when jurists perish, there perish also law and peace, and nothing remains but robbery, murder, outrage, and force—the reign of wild beasts. But what the merchant will gain when peace vanishes, I shall let his ledger tell him; and the use of all his property when preaching ceases, let his conscience show him.

It is a ground of special vexation that such foolish and unchristian language is used by those who pretend to be evangelical, and who know how to beat down every opponent with Scripture; and yet, at the same time, they do not bestow honor enough upon God or their chidren to educate them for these divine and exalted offices, through which they could serve their Maker and the world, and in which their temporal wants would be provided for. On the contrary, they turn their children away from these callings, and urge them to the service of Mammon, in which their success is uncertain, their bodies and souls are endangered, and their lives can in no way be considered a service of God.

I should mention here how many learned men are needed in medicine and the other professions, in reference to which a book might be written, and six months spent in preaching. Where would our preachers, jurists, and physicians come from, if the liberal arts were not taught? It is from this source they all must come. But to speak of this in detail would carry me too far. To be brief, an industrious, pious school-master or teacher, who faithfully trains and educates boys, can never be sufficiently recompensed, and no money will pay him, as even the heathen Aristotle says. Yet this calling is shamefully despised among us, as if it were nothing—and at the same time we pretend to be Christians!

If I had to give up preaching and my other duties, there is no office I would rather have than that of school-teacher. For I know that next to the ministry it is the most useful, greatest, and best; and I am not sure which of the two is to be preferred. For it is hard to make old dogs docile and old rogues pious, yet that is what the ministry works at, and must work at, in great part, in vain; but young trees, though some may break in the process, are more easily bent and trained. Therefore let it be considered one of the highest virtues on earth faithfully to train the children of others, which duty but very few parents attend to themselves.

That physicians in a sense become lords, is everywhere apparent; and that they can not be dispensed with, is taught by experience; but that medicine is a useful, comforting, and salutary profession, and likewise an acceptable and divinely appointed service of God, appears not only from the work itself, but also from Scripture. The thirty-eighth chapter of Ecclesiasticus is devoted to the praise of physicians: "Honor a physician with the honor due unto him for the uses which you may have of him; for the Lord hath created him. For of the Most High cometh healing. The Lord hath created medicines out of the earth; and he that is wise will not abhor them. Was not the water made sweet with wood, that the virtue thereof might be known? With such doth He heal men, and taketh away their pains. Of such doth the apothecary make a confection; and of his works there is no end," etc. But I am going too far; other preachers may develop these points more fully, and show the people better than I can write it, what injury or benefit may here be done the world and posterity.

Here I will leave the matter, faithfully admonishing and beseeching every one who can to help. For consider how many blessings God has bestowed upon you,—body, soul, house, wife, child, peace, the service and use of all His creatures in heaven and in earth—above all His Gospel and ministry, baptism, the Lord's Supper, and the whole treasure of His Son and Spirit, not only without any merit on your part, but also without cost or labor—and all bestowed in vain; for you support neither schools nor pastors, though according to the Gospel you are under obligation to do so; and besides, you show yourselves such accursed and ungrateful wretches that you are unwilling to give your sons to be educated for maintaining these gifts of God, but possess every thing in vain, not manifesting a drop of gratitude, but on the contrary letting the kingdom of God and the salvation of souls be neglected, to their destruction.

Ought not God to be angry? Ought not famine to come? Ought not pestilence, toil, the French, and other plagues, to find us out? Ought not savage tyrants to reign? Ought not war and strife to arise? Ought not bad government to prevail in the German states? Ought not Turks and Tartars to plunder us? Yea, it would be no wonder if God should open the doors and windows of hell, and let all the devils loose upon us, or if He should rain fire and brimstone from heaven and sink us all in the abyss of hell, as He did Sodom and Gomorrah. For if Sodom and Gomorrah had possessed, and heard, and seen as much as we have been blessed with, they would still exist at the present day. For they were ten times less guilty than Germany is now; for they did not have the Word of God and the ministry as we have them—but alas! in vain, since we act as if we wished that God, His Word, and all discipline and learning, might perish. And indeed factious spirits have actually begun to suppress God's Word, and the nobility and the rich are working to overthrow discipline and honor, that the people may suffer as they have deserved.

To have the Gospel and ministry, what else is it than the blood of our Lord? He secured it and presented it to us through His agonizing death on the cross. Yet we have it in vain, and have done and given nothing for it! O God, how bitterly did He suffer! and yet, how willingly! How much have the dear apostles and all the saints suffered for the Gospel, that it might be transmitted to us! How many in our own time have died for it!

And, to boast a little, how often have I been obliged to suffer the pains of death for the Gospel, that I might serve the German people—but my suffering is nothing in comparison with that of Christ, the Son of God; and yet He receives nothing further from our hands than that some persecute, condemn, and blaspheme this dearly-bought office; while others refuse to support the ministry, and give nothing to maintain that holy office. Moreover, they turn their children away from it, that the office may soon perish, and the sufferings and death of Christ become of no effect; at the same time, they live on in security, feel no compunctions of conscience for their more than diabolical ingratitude and utterly inexpressible sin, exhibit no fear of God's wrath, no love for the dear Saviour on account of His bitter sufferings, and yet, after such frightful wickedness, they pretend to be evangelical Christians!

If this deplorable blindness and sin were to continue in the German states, I should feel sorry that I was born in Germany and that I have spoken and written German; and if I could conscientiously do it, I would advise and help the Pope to rule over us again with all his abominations, and to oppress, flay, and destroy us, even beyond his former tyranny. Formerly, when the devil was served, and Christ's blood insulted, every purse was open, and there was no measure to the contributions made to churches, schools, and every abomination; then, too, people could urge and force their children into cloisters, chapters, churches, schools, with unspeakable cost—all of which was lost.

But now, when good schools and evangelical churches are to be established, nay, not established but merely maintained (for God has already established them, and given sufficient means for their support), when we know that we have God's Word, that evangelical churches are to be maintained, that Christ's sufferings and death are to be honored: now all purses are closed with iron chains, no one can give, and children are not even allowed to be supported by the Church, (where nothing is to be given,) and they are prevented from entering such salutary offices, in which their temporal wants would be provided for, and in which they would serve God and honor the blood of Christ; on the contrary, they are pushed into the jaws of Mammon, they tread the blood of Christ under foot, and yet pretend to be Christians!

I pray God to take me away, that I may never see the sorrow that is to come upon Germany. For I believe that if ten men like Moses stood before God and prayed for us, it would be of no avail; and when I pray for my dear Germany, I feel that my prayer rebounds, and does not ascend to heaven, as it does when I pray for other objects. God grant that I may be a false prophet! These disasters might be averted, if we would reform, and honor the Word of the Lord and the death of Christ as we have not hitherto done, and bring up the young to fill the various offices instituted by God.

But I maintain that the civil authorities are under obligation to compel the people to send their children to school, especially such as are promising, as has elsewhere been said. For our rulers are certainly bound to maintain the spiritual and secular offices and callings, so that there may always be preachers, jurists, pastors, scribes, physicians, school-masters, and the like; for these can not be dispensed with. If the government can compel such citizens as are fit for military service to bear spear and rifle, to mount ramparts, and perform other martial duties in time of war; how much more has it a right to compel the people to send their children to school, because in this case we are warring with the devil, whose object it is secretly to exhaust our cities and principalities of their strong men, to destroy the kernel and leave a shell of ignorant and helpless people, whom he can sport and juggle with at pleasure. That is starving out a city or country, destroying it without a struggle, and without its knowledge. The Turk does differently, and takes every third child in his empire to educate for whatever he pleases. How much more should our rulers require children to be sent to school, who, however, are not taken from their parents, but are educated for their own and the general good, in an office where they have an adequate support.

Therefore, let him who can, watch; and wherever the government sees a promising boy, let him be sent to school. If the father is poor, let the child be aided with the property of the Church. The rich should make bequests to such objects, as some have done, who have founded scholarships; that is giving money to the Church in a proper way. You do not thus release the souls of the dead from purgatorial fire, but you help, through the maintenance of divinely appointed offices, to prevent the living from going to purgatory—yea, you secure their deliverance from hell and entrance into heaven, and bestow upon them temporal peace and happiness. That would be a praiseworthy, Christian bequest, in which God would take pleasure, and for which He would honor and bless you, that you might have joy and peace in Him. Now, my dear Germans, I have warned you enough; you have heard your prophet. God grant that we may follow His Word, to the praise and honor of our dear Lord, for His precious blood so graciously shed for us, and preserve us from the horrible sin of ingratitude and forgetfulness of His benefits. Amen.

INDEX.

Alexander VI., character of, 16.
Ancient languages, 156, 183, 184; necessary to preserve the gospel, 186; helpful to ministers, 192; advantageous in ordinary life, 235.
Anselm, on method, 85.
Aristotle, Luther's dislike for, 102, 144; estimate of teachers, 264.
Asceticism, influence of, 75.
Augsburg Confession, on civil government, 63.
Battle hymn, Luther's, 96.
Bequests to education, 270.
Bible, practically prohibited by the Papacy, 44; weapon of the Reformers, 56; necessitates popular education, 61; an instrument of culture, 62, 63; difficulties of Luther in translating, 110; to be studied in schools, 147; requisites for teaching, 148; in what languages written, 185; to be studied, not in commentaries, but in the original, 189, 191.
Bismarck on Papal power, 35.
Boniface VIII., bull *Unam Sanctam*, 38.
Book of Concord, on rule of faith, 55.
Books, what kinds to be collected in libraries, 207.
Bréal, Michel, quoted, 62.
Brethren of Common Life, 85.
Bull, *In Cœna Domini*, 40.
Carlyle, on Luther, 112.
Catalogue, prohibitory, of Roman Catholic Church, 44.
Catechism, Luther's, 68; value in religious instruction, 121; principal parts of, 121; place in education, 148; how to be used, 150.

Celibacy, why rejected by the Reformers, 57.
Chaucer, description of a pardoner, 25.
Children, to be brought up for God, 116, 222; proper rearing of, a religious work, 117; how ruined by parents, 125; neglect of, denounced, 131; to be taught the Scriptures, 147; the catechism, 149; not to be perplexed with controversy, 153; the neglect of, a shame, 177; a sin, 178; why often neglected, 179; their pleasure in learning, 198; sermon on sending to school, 218-270; to be educated for the Church, 222; not all to be so educated, 234; what done with promising children, 235; to be educated for civil government, 244; raised to high positions by education, 260; poor children should be aided, 270.
Church, corruption of, 14; Papal definition of, 32; Roman organization of, 34; church and secular power in Protestantism, 57; helped by schools, 132; church fathers frequently misunderstood Scripture, 188.
Cities, their duty to maintain schools, 180; authorities urged to, 202.
Comenius, a fundamental educational principle of, 152.
Common sense, value and nature of, 101.
Council, Plenary, of Baltimore, 47; of Trent, on indulgences, 27; rule prohibiting the Bible, 44.
Councils, the reformatory, 22.
Courage, source of, 97.
Deharbe, on the Reformation, 11.
Devil, opposed to education, 171, 215; corrupted schools, 172; encourages the worship of Mammon, 211.
Diet of Spires, 52; of Worms, 53.
Discipline, domestic, 123; to be tempered with love, 123; rod not to be spared, 124.
Discoveries, relation of, to Reformation, 13.
Dittes, on Luther's pedagogy, 67.
Domestic training, 113-117; the basis of social order, 114; a divine requirement, 116; a religious work, 117; reasons

INDEX. 275

for, 118; difficulties of, 119; in spiritual things, 120; home discipline, 123; the soul more than the body, 124; three faults of, 125; sum of filial duty, 126; Luther's high ideal, 126.

Duty, filial, the sum of, 126.

Education, popular, and the Papacy, 32–51; and Protestantism, 52–74; science of, due to Protestantism, 66; in Roman and Protestant countries, 70; beginning of, in the United States, 71; fundamental difference between Protestant and Papal, 72; before the Reformation, 75–89; secular education in Middle Ages, 79; knightly education, 80; burgher schools, 81; female education in the Middle Ages, 81; condition of, at beginning of the sixteenth century, 83; in the family, 113–127; in spiritual things, 120; to be made a pleasure, 122; how advanced by Luther, 128; neglect of, denounced, 131; two great reasons for, 131; compulsory, 136, 269; comprehends three classes of schools, 138; for girls, 138, 196; public better than private, 141, 197; definitions of, 145; studies and methods in, 147–168; place of Scripture in, 147; of catechism, 149; Socratic method, 152; to be adapted to child nature, 154; the concrete to illustrate the abstract, 155; ancient languages in, 156; the mother tongue, 157; rhetoric and logic, 159; history, 160; natural science, 162; music, 164; gymnastics, 166; importance of education, 173; reasons for supporting, 174; a divine command, 176; neglect of, a shame, 177; also a sin, 178; value of, to cities, 181; to civil order, 196; evils of neglecting, 216, 224, 232.

Eloquence, nature of, 107.

Erasmus, lack of martyr spirit, 95; indifferent to nature, 163.

Faith, justification by, 57; how viewed by Luther, 58; brings the soul into immediate relation to God, 59; an element of strength, 96.

Famines, various, referred to, 240.

Fathers, Church, frequently misunderstood the Scriptures, 188.

Fredet, mutilation of history, 43.
Gallicanism, 33.
Germans, religious nature of, 22 ; fundamental traits of character, 91.
Germany, condition of, 176; source of civil law, 245; Luther's fears for, 269.
Gerson, on method, 85.
Gladstone, on Papal power, 35.
God in history, 26; enjoins education, 176.
Good works, in Romanism and Protestantism, contrasted, 231.
Government, civil, a divine ordinance, 63, 243; Luther on, 134; schools to be maintained for, 135; needs schools, 194, 196; ministerial and civil office compared, 242.
Grammar, office of, 158.
Greeks, example in education, 195.
Gregory VII., on Papal power, 22.   Gregory XVI. quoted, 42.
Groot, Gerhard, 85.
Guizot, on the Reformation, 12.
Gymnastics, 166.
Hegel, on the Reformation, 14.
Heroes of an epoch, 90.
Historians, utility and character of, 161.
History, supplies illustrations, 155 ; shows God's dealings with men, 160.
Hosmer on Luther as philosopher and poet, 104.
Hymns of Luther, 105 ; Coleridge on, 105 ; a Jesuit's testimony, 105.
Index expurgatorius, 44.
Indulgences, doctrine of, 26, 27; Council of Trent on, 27; sale of, by Tetzel, 28.
Janssen, Johannes, quoted, 86.
Jesuits, maxim of, in education, 50; reason for their educational activity, 50.
Judgment Day, 233.
Justification by faith, 57; how viewed by Luther, 58; brings the soul into immediate relation to God, 59.

Justinian quoted, 254.
Knights, education of, 80; knights and scribes compared, 258; knightly order not to be undervalued, 259.
Knowledge, of two kinds, 158.
Languages, ancient, 156, 183: necessary to preserve the Gospel, 186; helpful to ministers, 192; advantageous in ordinary life, 235.
Leo X., remark of, 15; Maximilian's estimate of his character, 24.
Lessing, on Luther, 98.
Libraries, 203; origin of, 203; bad books in, 205; what books to collect, 206.
Literature, attitude of, toward the Papacy, 24.
Logic, office of, 159.
Luther, ninety-five theses, 29; at Worms, 53; on justification by faith, 58; religious experience, 58; on priesthood of believers, 60; letter to mayors and aldermen in behalf of Christian schools, 67, 169; pedagogy of, 67; his catechisms, 68, 88; establishes schools at Eisleben, 68; on popular ignorance, 88; chapter on, 90; the hero of the sixteenth century, 91; his early career and ability, 92; called to Wittenberg, 94; fitness for his work, 94; honesty of character, 95; a man of faith, 96; courage of, 97; violence of, 98; his style in writing, 100, 111; intellectual strength, 101; æsthetic tastes, 102; tenderness of, 103; as a poet, 104; domestic life, 106; at his daughter's death-bed, 107; his eloquence, 108; conservative character, 108; industry, 109; apology to his printer, 110; his toil in translating the Bible, 110; summary of his character, 111; Carlyle on, 112; on domestic training, 113-127; on marriage, 113; on filial obedience, 114; on the parental relation, 115; who should marry, 119; on religious instruction, 120; on domestic discipline, 123; on schools, 128-146; how he advanced education, 128; on the establishment of schools, 129; fundamental reasons for schools, 131; on the ministerial

office, 133, 218-222; opposed to secularizing schools, 136; favored compulsory education, 136, 269; three classes of schools, 138; on female education, 138, 196, 200; on school training, 141, 197; on teacher's vocation, 142; ministers should first be teachers, 143; on ministers, 144, conception of education, 145; on studies and methods, 147-168; on the study of Scripture, 147; qualifications for teaching Scripture, 148; on the use of the catechism, 149; children not to be perplexed with controversy, 153; a student of child-nature, 154; the concrete to be used to illustrate the abstract, 155; on the ancient lauguages, 156, 183; a teacher of the mother tongue, 157; method in language teaching, 157; on rhetoric and logic, 159; on pedantry, 160; on history, 160; appreciation of nature, 162; love of music, 164; on gymnastics, 166; summary of educational merits, 167; confidence in his mission, 170; boasts of the Spirit, 193; children's delight in learning, 198; on libraries, 203-208; on evils of neglecting education, 224; on civil government, 242, 243; praises his craft, 254; a beggar pupil, 261; school teaching next to preaching, 264; his fears for Germany, 269.

Macaulay, contrast of Papal and Protestant countries, 50; on poets, 104.

Mammon, worship of, hurtful to education, 213; depreciates culture, 262.

Marriage, Luther on, 113; who should marry, 119.

Mass, why rejected, 56; false honor of celebrating, 220.

Massacre of St. Bartholomew misrepresented, 43.

Maximilian, Emperor, quoted, 259.

McCarthy, on public schools, 46.

McGlynn, Rev. Dr., quoted, 49.

Melanchthon, on popular ignorance, 87; on Luther's eloquence, 108; the Zwickau prophets, 109.

Methods, of teaching, 147-168; how to use the catechism, 150; fundamental principle of Comenius, 152; Socratic

INDEX. 279

method, 152; children not to be perplexed with controversies, 153; teaching to be adapted to child-nature, 154; learning to be made pleasant, 154; the concrete to illustrate the abstract, 155; in teaching language, 157; children's delight in learning, to be utilized, 198; study and labor to be combined, 199.

Meyer, testimony of, 18.

Middle Ages, education during, 75-89; not to be unduly depreciated, 75; character of, 76; courses of study, 77; educational defects, 83; character of teachers, 84; common people neglected, 86.

Milton, definition of education, 145.

Ministers, first to be teachers, 143; all do not need the highest culture, 190; should urge education, 212, 213, 217; letter to, 215; their worth, 229; support for, 237; lack of, 238.

Ministry, value of, 133; ordained of God, 218, 219; duties of, 219; to be honored, 221; great works of, 224; benefits to society, 228, 229; support of, 237.

Monasteries, condition of, 17; multiplication of, 76; benefits of, 77; defective instruction, 175.

Music, Luther's praise of, 164.

Myconius, description of religious life under the Papacy, 20.

National feeling, growth of, 24.

Nature, as viewed by Protestantism, 65, 66.

Neander, on the mediæval clergy, 79.

Niemeyer, definition of education, 145.

Nuremburg, excellent school of, 211.

Oath of Papal clergy, 35.

Obedience, Luther on, 114.

Papacy, dissoluteness of, 15; legalism, 17; persecutions by, 19, 23; historical development of, 21, 22; pretension to temporal power, 22, 37; Babylonish captivity of, 24; relation to education, 32-51; divisions of, 33; primacy over the world, 34; opposed to American institutions, 36; doctrine and discipline of, 36, 37; reactionary character, 39; opposed to religious freedom, 39; aims at universal supremacy, 40; attitude of, toward Protestantism, 40; opposed to intellectual freedom, 42; prohibits the Bible, 44; seeks control of the young, 45; attitude toward public schools, 46; unfavorable to popular education, 49; requires a mediating priesthood, 58.

Parental relation, 115.

Parents, selfish, neglect education, 171; why they neglect it, 179; responsibility of, 232; share in their children's honor, 247; God's requirements of, 249; shame in neglecting education, 249; should educate in faith, 261; an appeal to, 265.

Pedantry, condemned, 160.

Physicians, value of, 264.

Pius IX., warning against Protestant literature, 43.

Poets, character of, 104; Macaulay on, 104; Shakespeare on, 104.

Preachers, see Ministers.

Priesthood, mediating, 58; of believers, 59; views of Luther on, 60; Protestant view of, emancipating the laity, 60.

Protestantism and popular education, 52–74; origin of name, 52; misrepresented by Papists, 54; fundamental principles of, 55; gives the Bible to laity, 61; dignifies life, 64; makes education an interest of Church and State, 64; favors the study of nature, 65; the mother of popular education, 74.

Rambler (Catholic), on religions liberty, 41.

Reformation, causes of, 9–31; interests affected by, 9, 10; a subject of controversy, 10; Voltaire's view, 10; Roman view, 11; in relation to schools, 67.

Religion, a personal relation to Christ, 17.

Revival of learning, 13.

Rhetoric, to be studied, 159.

Roman Catholic statistics, 48; institutions in New York, 48.

Rome, education in ancient, 181; example in education, 195.

Saxony, School Plan, 68.

Schiphower, on monastic life, 17.

INDEX. 281

Schmid, on Protestant and Papal education, 72.
Scholars, pleasures of, 251; worth not appreciated, 256.
Schools, monastic, 76, 200; cathedral and parochial, 78; burgher schools, 81; methods of instruction in Middle Ages, 83; character of teachers, 84; condition of, at beginning of sixteenth century, 87; Luther on, 128-146; why to be established, 129; helpful to the Church, 132; necessary for the State, 135; not to be secularized, 136; to be maintained by the civil authorities, 137; three kinds contemplated by Luther, 138; schools for girls, 138; school training better than private instruction, 141; studies in, 147-168; Scriptures, 147; catechism, 149; controversies to be avoided in, 153; the concrete to illustrate the abstract, 155; ancient languages in, 156; decline of schools, 170; reasons for supporting, 174: defects of Papal schools, 206; results of neglecting, 216, 232.
Sermon on sending children to school, 218-270.
Shakespeare, on poetic genius, 104.
Smalcald Articles, quoted, 58.
Society, constitution of, 114.
Socratic method, 152.
Soldiers, conceited, despise culture, 255.
Spencer, Herbert, definition of education, 145.
Spengler, Lazarus, letter to, 210.
Spires, Diet of, 52.
Strack, quoted, 84.
Strong, Dr. Josiah, quoted, 49.
Studies, Luther on, 147-168: Scriptures of chief importance, 147; catechism, 149; ancient languages, 156; the mother tongue, 157; rhetoric and logic, 159; history, 160; natural sciences, 162; music, 164; gymnastics, 166; study and labor to be combined, 199.
Study, course of, in Middle Ages, 77.
Syllabus of Errors, on temporal power, 38; condemns religious toleration, 40; condemns public schools, 46.

Teachers, in Middle Ages, 84; qualifications for teaching Scripture, 148; not appreciated, 263.
Teaching, an honorable calling, 142, 264.
Tetzel, sale of indulgences, and blasphemies, 28.
Thirty-nine Articles on rule of faith, 56.
Ultramontanism, character of, 33; in relation to temporal power, 37.
Unam Sanctam, bull, 38.
Universities, rise of, 82; great number of students, 82; four faculties, 83; needed reformation, 144; defective instruction of, 175.
Vatican Council, decrees of, 34.
Voltaire, on the Reformation, 10.
Votes, Roman Catholic, 48.
Waldenses, neglect of languages, 156, 194.
Walther von der Vogelweide, quoted, 25.
Words *versus* things, 158.
Zwickau prophets, 109.

www.ingramcontent.com/pod-product-compliance
Lightning Source LLC
Chambersburg PA
CBHW032037150426
43194CB00006B/316